Deliberative Democracy

Deliberative Democracy

A Critical Introduction

Zsuzsanna Chappell

First published 2012 by
PALGRAVE MACMILLAN

Palgrave Macmillan in the UK is an imprint of Macmillan Publishers
Limited, registered in England, company number 785998, of Houndmills,
Basingstoke, Hampshire RG21 6XS.

Palgrave Macmillan in the US is a division of St Martin's Press LLC,
175 Fifth Avenue, New York, NY 10010.

Palgrave Macmillan is the global academic imprint of the above companies
and has companies and representatives throughout the world.

Palgrave® and Macmillan® are registered trademarks in the United States,
the United Kingdom, Europe and other countries

ISBN 978–0–230–25215–8 hardback
ISBN 978–0–230–25216–5 paperback

This book is printed on paper suitable for recycling and made from fully
managed and sustained forest sources. Logging, pulping and manufacturing
processes are expected to conform to the environmental regulations of the
country of origin.

A catalogue record for this book is available from the British Library.

A catalog record for this book is available from the Library of Congress.

10   9   8   7   6   5   4   3   2   1
21 20 19 18 17 16 15 14 13 12

Printed in China

Contents

List of Tables and Figures

Tables

Figures

Acknowledgements

It would not have been possible to write this book without the help of family, friends, colleagues and students. I would like to thank Christian List, Keith Dowding, Chandran Kukathas and Richard Bellamy, without whom I would not have received a PhD, let alone completed this book. Many others have given me feedback on part of this work, discussed some of the material with me or simply encouraged me to just get on with writing. These include Brian Barry, Adrian Blau, Kim Brownlee, Philip Cook, John Dryzek, Stephen Elstub, Esha Senchaudhuri, Jessica Templeton, James Wong and Stephen de Wijze. I have learnt a lot from participants of three seminar groups I have been privileged to be part of: the Political Theory Group and the Choice Group at the London School of Economics and the Manchester Centre for Political Theory (MANCEPT) at the University of Manchester. I would like to thank my students, both at the London School of Economics and the University of Manchester, for making me articulate my thoughts more clearly. It would have been impossible to complete this book without the excellent work and kindly reminders of my editors, Steven Kennedy, Stephen Wenham and Helen Caunce, as well as Keith Povey (with Nancy Richardson), who supervised the final stages of the book's production. I have received very helpful feedback from the two anonymous reviewers.

I would also like to thank those who helped me in practical ways while I was completing this book; in particular Patrizia Collard, Aditi Jain and Mervi Pitkanen. Last but not least, I would like to thank my husband Gerald for encouraging me and putting up with me when I was being insufferable.

ZSUZSANNA CHAPPELL

1
Introduction

The word deliberation can conjure up many different images. It might remind us of the decisions of juries and judges, a lone individual weighing up which way he or she should act, learned discussion between scientists or heated debate amongst politicians. Yet over the last few decades another conception of deliberation has become prominent in political theory: that of *democratic* deliberation.

All theories of politics have to address some of the same fundamental questions. How can a group of people with a plurality of preferences and beliefs decide on what laws to follow and how to allocate scarce resources? The way that such collective decisions are made needs to be legitimate; that is, individuals subject to it should be able to endorse the decision-making process and accept the decisions that it produces. The theory of deliberative democracy aims to achieve this kind of legitimacy through democratic deliberation.

Imagine the following scenario. It is an ordinary working day in the country of Democratia. Except for one thing: most adult citizens will at some point during the day visit a polling station to vote in an election that determines who will govern their country for the next four years. They will take public transport, drive or walk, they will queue up and have their name crossed off a register. Then they will stand on their own in a cubicle with a small piece of paper that allows them to make an extraordinary decision. Each voting citizen will have the right to proclaim on his or her ballot paper who should govern the country and how. This individual choice will then be counted, together with all the choices other voters have made, and each citizen has a small slice of power that enables him or her to have a say in how the country is run. Late at night or early next morning, a winner is declared, who is now authorized to govern the country legitimately.

1

But is this all there is to democracy? And should we not demand more of our democracies? Imagine another scenario. It is an ordinary Saturday, but a group of citizens is not pursuing their ordinary daily lives in the country of Democratia. Instead, this weekend they are meeting to discuss an issue affecting their community. They will study the facts available. They will listen to each other carefully and weigh arguments for and against their available options. Everyone is an equal in this group and no one is treated disrespectfully. If no unanimous decision is reached by the end of the day, a vote is taken. Whatever they choose can now be seen as a legitimate decision. This kind of collective decision-making is the basis of the theory of deliberative democracy.

The theory and practice of democracy have evolved substantially over time. Over the last hundred years democracy has been extended both in its breadth, territorially, and in its depth, through the extension of the franchise and increased transparency in politics. According to Freedom House (2011), at the end of 2010 there existed 87 free and democratic states, nearly half of the 194 independent states in the world. Over the last century, democracy has also been deepened considerably in established democracies, through the introduction of universal suffrage, campaign finance reforms and measures aimed at eradicating corruption and increasing transparency.

The question is: in what direction should the theory and practice of democracy now evolve? The most prominent trend in democratic thought is for extending the scope of democratic politics by making democracy more *deliberative*. Over the last twenty-odd years, the literature on the theory of deliberative democracy has expanded rapidly, followed by a growing number of empirical studies on deliberation.

The theory of deliberative democracy argues that the essence of democratic politics does not lie in voting and representation. Instead, its essence is the common deliberation that should underlie collective decision making. This theory shifts the focus to the debate that needs to take place between citizens in order to make reasoned and considered decisions, whether these take place between groups of citizens, in the legislature or in the wider public sphere. Such political discussions are intended to make citizens take into account the perspectives and needs of others in society. They move the emphasis of democratic politics from contestation to common problem solving.

What is Wrong with Democracy?

Deliberative democrats respond to a conception of politics as adversarial contest. They are also prompted by the view that there is something wrong with democracy as it exists now. Thus they respond both to trends in theorizing about democracy and to current practices in real-world democracies.

Much of political science depicts democracy as an essentially adversarial process by focusing primarily on competitive elections. Other important models of democracy – agonism, elite theory, pluralism – all have their basis in this competitive aspect. Agonism defines politics itself as unavoidably conflictual (Honig 1993; Mouffe 1993, 1996, 2005). Elite theorists, such as Schumpeter (1976), have based this contestation among elected politicians, while the vast majority of citizens only have a nominal say in collective decisions. Pluralism, probably the most influential theory of democracy before the deliberative one arose, places it in the hands of competing interest groups. Deliberative democrats argue that this focus is misplaced and it is reasoned discussion and a search for agreement that should guide us instead.

Deliberative democrats are equally dissatisfied with those political scientists who approach the study of democracy from the rational choice-theoretic perspective that is often described as the application of economic principles to the study of politics. These studies adopt the assumption from economics that individuals are utility maximizers: they act in a way that will secure them the outcome they most wish for. Individuals choose actions which, according to their beliefs, will lead them to satisfy their preferences. Thus, if I want a cup of tea I know that the way to get this is by going to the kitchen and putting the kettle on, therefore I will choose to do so.

There is a very large literature in political science that produces increasingly sophisticated rational choice-theoretic models (Dennis Mueller (2003) provides an excellent and very detailed survey of the field in *Public Choice III*). These cover a wide range of topics including electoral competition (Downs 1957; Besley and Coate 1991), redistribution (Meltzer and Richard 1981; Husted and Kenny 1997), models of bureaucracies (Niskanen 1971; Dunleavy 1991) and legislatures (Cox and McCubbins 1993; Laver and Shepsle 1995; Tsebelis 2002).

On a more abstract level, social choice theory (Arrow 1951/1963; Riker 1982; Sen 1970) is the study of how voting rules can achieve fair results that reflect the preferences of individual voters as accurately as possible. It is thus one of the main targets of deliberative democrats. Social choice-theoretic results indicate that it is impossible to find a voting rule or way of counting votes that fulfils a relatively small number of democratic values simultaneously (see also Chapter 5). The most famous of these is Arrow's theorem (1951/1963), but such results have been extended to aggregating judgements rather than preferences (List and Pettit 2002) and to showing that no vote-counting rule is immune to manipulation (Gibbard 1973, Satterthwaite 1975). A significant part of social choice theory is concerned with relaxing various conditions in order to overcome these impossibility results.

Different electoral rules will result in different outcomes and in view of the impossibility results, no 'best' electoral rule exists. Therefore, according to Riker (1982), one of the best-known proponents of these theories, the indeterminate and arbitrary nature of electoral outcomes means that the general will cannot exist. Elections are therefore a mechanism for removing 'bad' officials, rather than a manifestation of the popular will.

Most deliberative democrats argue that these approaches to the study of democracy and politics are too limited. They do not pay sufficient attention to the non-selfish, 'other-regarding' aspect of politics. By focusing on given individual preferences, so the critics say, rational and social choice theorists neglect the way in which these preferences are formed. Other deliberative democrats seek to reconcile deliberative democracy with social choice theory (Dryzek and List 2003) and rational choice theory (Fung 2004).

The theory of deliberative democracy also responds to the problems that currently exist in democratic practice. These include apathetic, badly informed voters, low turnout, elections fought with sound-bite rhetoric and political exclusion. Newer democracies also experience more severe problems of corruption and a relative lack of transparency in political decision making. But for now let us focus on well-established, stable democratic systems.

There is a large survey-based literature that shows that citizens in developed democracies know very little about politics. American citizens are more likely to know the name of the president's dog than his stance on capital punishment (Delli Carpini and Keeter 1996). The question arises how such badly informed voters can be useful participants in the democratic process and whether they can be good citizens at all. In order to make sense of politics and to make choices in elections, most citizens use heuristic cues, such as the party affiliations of candidates (Popkin 1993). As a result, it is often felt that political contests, especially in the United States, are increasingly fought with simple rhetoric and aggressive attacks on opponents. Thus, from the perspective of deliberative democrats, current politics are neither reasoned, nor based on facts and accurate information.

But even the information that citizens do receive is often biased. Most of the media present issues in strongly partisan terms, and people are most likely to choose news sources which will confirm their existing ideological views (Campbell *et al.* 1960). This tendency is reinforced by the Internet, which is fast becoming an important source of news and political commentary (Sunstein 2007). While it is possible to access traditional news sources, such as broadsheet newspapers, radio and television online, there are also a very large number of highly partisan and biased news websites and blogs. In accessing these, citizens will not be exposed to the points of view of others in society and will not learn enough about the interests of others to take these into consideration when they make political decisions.

Other studies have reported a decrease in civic participation. The best-known such study is Putnam's *Bowling Alone* (2000), an influential book which highlighted the fact that Americans are now less likely to be members of groups and associations such as PTAs, bowling clubs or even churches than they were in previous decades. This results in a loss of what Putnam calls *social capital*, the number of networks and relationships that people are part of in society. Instead, they participate in civic life through large, 'cheque-book' organizations and socialize with close friends and family. This means that citizens are less likely to get to know and learn about others around them and be exposed to other points of view. There is also some evidence that this may make citizens less likely to participate in politics, as they are not mobilized to do so through interacting with civic associations.

Most citizens do not participate in resource-intensive political activities, such as writing to their representatives, campaigning, attending demonstrations, signing petitions or standing for office. An increasing number of citizens do not even vote in elections. Instead, many citizens appear to be uninterested in politics. They feel that their political efficacy is low; they believe that even if they did participate, this would not make a difference. According to the annual study carried out by the UK's Electoral Commission (Electoral

Commission and Hansard Society 2007), 32 per cent of British citizens feel they are too busy to participate in politics, 22 per cent are too uninterested to do so, 6 per cent feel their participation would not achieve anything, 2 per cent feel they would not be listened to and 17 per cent of citizens do not even know why they do not participate. The same study found that 19 per cent of citizens had not voted or participated in politics for the previous two or three years. These figures do not change significantly over time (Electoral Commission and Hansard Society 2011). Furthermore, the majority of citizens are not interested in participating more than they currently do, and many of those who claim they would like to do so exaggerate the likelihood of their starting to participate in the future (Electoral Commission and Hansard Society 2011). These results are echoed by the results of a survey carried out in the US over fifteen years earlier (Verba *et al.* 1995). In this study 39 per cent of citizens cited time as the reason for not participating, 17 per cent felt politics was too boring, 15 per cent thought they would have no impact and 19 per cent had never even thought of taking part in politics.

It is not only that citizens are apathetic, too busy or disillusioned when it comes to politics. Both of the above studies show that there are statistically significant variations in the likelihood that someone will participate in politics depending on income, education, socio-economic status and race. Thus those who are better educated and better off dominate politics. Education is the single highest predictor of political participation, but is itself correlated with other factors such as income or socio-economic status (Verba *et al.* 1995, Perrin 2006). As Schattschneider famously put it, 'the flaw in the pluralist heaven is that the heavenly chorus sings with a strong upper-class accent' (Schattschneider 1960, p.35). Thus current democratic systems tend to include some groups more in political decision making than others, while at the margins citizens can face political exclusion.

There appears to be much that is wrong with contemporary liberal democracies. Deliberative democracy is aimed at making all citizens more involved and better informed and politicians more open and accountable. Thus deliberative democrats display a strong concern for improving both the theory of democracy, by strengthening its normative foundations and making it less adversarial, and the practice of democracy, by finding practical ways in which day-to-day democratic politics can be made to resemble the ideal more closely.

Defining Deliberative Democracy

This newer theory is not simply about deliberation, but *political* and *democratic* deliberation. For my present purposes, I will define democratic deliberation as un-coerced, other-regarding, reasoned, inclusive and equal debate. This definition leaves open many questions about exact institutional arrangements and the practical limits of deliberative democracy. It does not tell us whether all issues should be decided through deliberation or only some, whether deliberation should take place locally, nationally or even globally and whether all citizens need to participate in it in order for democracy to be termed deliberative. However, it encapsulates the most important normative commitments of deliberative democrats, regardless of the topic, participants, exact rules and setting of deliberation.

Deliberation is political inasmuch as it aims to solve problems to which we need to respond collectively, whether these are moral issues or issues of distributing scarce resources in society (Christiano 1996). Furthermore, deliberation is democratic if it includes all substantively affected citizens and all relevant arguments to a sufficient degree and if it does so by guaranteeing at least minimal equality between them. I will now give a brief overview of these values, but their definition will be developed in more detail in the coming chapters.

Perhaps the most important commitment of deliberative democrats is to *reciprocal, other-regarding* debate. This reciprocal quality of deliberation is grounded in the requirement to give reasons and justifications for our beliefs in the political forum. This presupposes respect for other citizens that is manifested by providing them with reasons for our beliefs and preferences and by listening to the reasons they in turn provide. The underlying assumption is that in the public, political forum citizens and politicians need to justify their stand on issues in a way that others will understand, if not necessarily accept.

Deliberative democracy is also aimed at making citizens more other-regarding: more concerned about the interests of others and less selfish. This captures the intuition that in politics citizens should take the needs and interests of others into account when they form their preferences and contribute to making decisions. According to the theory, during deliberation citizens will learn about the perspectives, beliefs and interests of others to a much greater extent than they would be able to under more adversarial forms of democracy.

Offering reciprocal justifications also makes deliberative democracy more *reasoned*. Thus, the aim is to make collective decisions that take all relevant arguments into account and that are carefully considered rather than hasty. Deliberation also serves as an important source of information and thereby facilitates learning. It helps citizens acquire new information and correct false beliefs.

Reason giving also establishes the epistemic justifications of deliberative democracy. According to these, deliberative democracy is a good and desirable procedure, because it is good at tracking the truth (Peter 2007a). David Estlund (1997, 2008) endorses a form of deliberativism based on such epistemic grounds. His epistemic proceduralism states that while not perfect, democratic procedures are good at arriving at the truth or the best outcome, therefore we have grounds for obeying laws created through these procedures even when we believe them to be wrong. According to his definition, democracy and deliberation derive their epistemic advantage from individuals talking to each other, since 'two heads are better than one' (Estlund 2008: 177).

Another epistemic defence of deliberative democracy comes from pragmatist quarters. Pragmatists such as Misak (2000) and Talisse (2005) argue that the value of deliberative democracy lies in creating an ongoing debate in search of the truth that satisfies the requirements of pragmatic inquiry.

Thus, reasoned debate is valuable both from a procedural and from an outcome-based viewpoint. From the procedural point of view, it helps political decision-making processes to honour the seriousness of making decisions that affect a whole community. From the outcome-based point of view, requiring deliberation to be reasoned is the foundation of the epistemic justification of democracy.

What makes citizens reasonable is a controversial question. The deliberative democracy literature usually takes Rawls's concept of public reason (1993) as the standard of reasonableness in public debate (see Chapter 2). Some theorists (Fish 1999; Talisse 2005) criticize authors such as Gutmann and Thompson (1996, 2004) for holding conceptions of the reasonable that are much too narrow and will therefore exclude religious or illiberal views. Others (Young 2000) argue that reasonableness should not be a function of individuals' beliefs, but instead of their attitudes towards other deliberators. Thus, reasonable individuals are willing to engage in debate, offer public justifications for their preferences and reflect on their positions. By contrast, unreasonable citizens are unwilling to listen to others or even consider that their own position may be wrong.

The third normative value of deliberative democracy is *inclusiveness*. Thus, while in current democratic systems some individuals and groups are excluded from politics despite formal means of inclusion, such as providing each person with one vote, deliberative democrats seek to include all members of the community in the decision-making process. Moreover, deliberation should not only be inclusive of persons, but also of ideas, with all relevant arguments adequately represented during deliberative debates.

The inclusive aspect of deliberative democracy is emphasized particularly by so-called difference democrats such as Iris Young (1996, 2000). Their concern for inclusion originates from the need to give a voice to all citizens during deliberation and not to marginalize any groups by making it a privilege of the elites. In order to facilitate inclusion, political deliberation must not resemble a debating club, but should rather acknowledge and encourage various forms of communication between citizens (Young 2000). Thus, narratives and rhetoric must play an important role alongside logic and reasoning.

Deliberative democracy could be used as a tool to combat existing social injustices and political exclusion by giving those who are currently disadvantaged a voice and requiring the rest of society to listen. It could allow all citizens to present their perspectives, beliefs and interests to others, thereby enabling citizens and groups to find out more about each other. Deliberation could thus serve as a powerful means of increasing political inclusion and counteracting existing power differences in society.

Concern for equality is closely related to concern for inclusion. Despite formal equality among citizens, not all have equal power in current democracies. Without countering problems of inequality, deliberative democracy may make this situation worse if the better educated and those with higher incomes dominate the debate. Not all citizens may be able to participate in deliberation alike, as they may not have the necessary skills to present their arguments persuasively. Or they may not have the necessary resources, such as free time or money to attend meetings.

Therefore, many deliberative democrats argue for more substantive equality between citizens (Bohman 1997; Knight and Johnson 1997) as a precondition of equal deliberation. This could include making sure that all citizens have adequate capabilities to participate in democratic deliberation and to influence the political process. Thus, some deliberative democrats argue for better education and increased material equality to ensure that politics can be truly equal. However, the 'equality of what' debate does carry over into the deliberative democracy literature and there is no consensus on what we should equalize – resources, primary goods or capabilities – or how equality can be secured in a deliberative context (see Chapter 4).

The above values provide a good picture of the conception of politics that deliberative democrats promote. By using these values, they oppose adversarial or aggregative theories of democracy and respond to weaknesses in current practices of democracy. There are other values that are sometimes used to define deliberative democracy in the literature, such as that of aiming for a consensual decision (Cohen 1989), but deliberative democracy can be sufficiently defined without these. The values I have outlined above capture the essence of deliberative democracy and all deliberative democrats endorse them in some form, no matter what their disagreements over other questions may be. There is no such agreement over the need to aim for a consensus or the role that self-regarding preferences can play in deliberation.

Two Models of Deliberation

Micro deliberation

Within the theory of deliberative democracy, we can distinguish between two practical forms of deliberation: micro and macro deliberation. It is easy to imagine a micro deliberative scenario. It bears a strong resemblance to the group discussions that most of us attend at various times: seminars, committee meetings and the like. We can think of equivalents to these in politics even without explicit reference to new deliberative ideas. Talk and discussion are the guiding mechanisms behind the work of legislatures, committees and town hall meetings, even though the quality of that talk may not reach deliberative ideals. Many of the examples mentioned in this chapter and all of the examples I will return to in Chapter 6 are also of the micro deliberative variety. That is because to begin with, deliberative democrats focused on micro deliberation in order to develop their new model of democracy (Gutmann and Thompson 1996; Ackermann and Fishkin 2004; Fung 2003, 2004; Fishkin 2009).

Involving more citizens in reasoned discussion about political issues serves to enhance the legitimacy of democratic decision making through ensuring that citizens hold well-informed, thoughtfully formed preferences on issues. Micro deliberation usually takes place face-to-face. It is held at a clearly definable time and place, between well-defined participants. It is easy to observe who participates, how many times they talk and for how long and whether they keep to the rules of the deliberative encounter. What is said and whether a decision has been made can also be recorded. This makes it easy to apply rules to micro deliberative meetings that closely follow the normative values of the ideal theory (Chappell 2010).

However, micro deliberation also faces constraints. In order to ensure success, it is best if the topic of deliberation has been well defined in advance. This presupposes some form of agenda-setting process separate from the deliberative process itself. Given that it consists of face-to-face discussion, the number of participants also needs to be limited. It is impossible for a modern city, let alone for a modern nation state to participate in one giant micro deliberative debate simultaneously. Finally, micro deliberation is time-consuming and is not a by-product of other social or political activities.

While it is relatively easy to define what micro deliberation would look like, at the same time there can also be great differences between such micro deliberative events. They could be held on the local, regional, national or even international level. They can consist of a series of meetings or just one. Their participants may be experts, politicians or ordinary citizens. Their purpose might be to make a recommendation, arrive at a decision or simply to explore an issue.

The ideal standards of deliberative democracy apply straightforwardly to micro deliberation, even if they cannot be fully met under non-ideal circumstances. Other-regardingness may be self-reinforcing in small-group discussion, as entirely self-regarding arguments will simply be unconvincing to others. Inclusion can be more or less guaranteed by ensuring that the method used to select participants – whether sampling, invitation or self-selection – provides fair access to all affected persons, and by making sure that none are marginalized or excluded from the subsequent debate. Equality can be ensured in a variety of ways, including giving each speaker an equal speaking time or an equal chance to talk, should they wish to do so. It is harder to devise rules that ensure that deliberation is reasoned. It is, however, relatively easy to determine whether micro deliberation has conformed to these standards.

Especially when they are organized explicitly according to the principles of deliberative democracy, micro deliberative events often employ moderators in order to make sure that these normative principles are upheld in practice. The role of moderators is to facilitate the debate, to ensure equality and inclusion and to give guidance that encourages reasoned debate without determining the direction the discussion will take. This may be especially helpful in ensuring that the discussion is reasoned and other-regarding.

Thus micro deliberation can be seen as an archetype of democratic deliberation. Furthermore, it is easier to identify and study than macro deliberation. For a long time, therefore, micro deliberation has been implicitly or explicitly the main focus of study for democratic theorists. But advances in the theory and a recognition that a truly deliberative democracy needs to incorporate deliberation more broadly into its preference-forming, belief-forming and decision-making structures has led to an increased focus on macro deliberation in the public sphere.

Macro deliberation

Macro deliberation is the ongoing, disaggregated process of discussion in the public sphere. It takes place over a long period of time, not necessarily continuously. It encompasses many of the things we regard as necessary for a healthy democratic culture and civil society: free media, public debate, statements by politicians and the voice of civil society activists. All members of a polity can participate in macro deliberation should they wish to do so, although the extent of the opportunities they have for participation will vary considerably.

Macro deliberation has several important functions in democratic systems. Firstly, this is where new issues and possible solutions to them emerge. Thus, it has an important agenda-setting role. A democratic public sphere allows citizens to voice their concerns about collective problems. Freedom of association allows citizens to form groups aimed at advancing common interests in public. The media and mass communication allow these groups to reach out to others and to find out about the concerns of these other groups in turn. Those with particular interest in an issue can alert their fellow citizens to problems with the way in which they are governed and thus serve as whistle-blowers.

Macro deliberation can also serve to identify a reasonable set of solutions to collective problems. Public sphere debate can point out courses of action that are morally unacceptable, that would seriously hurt the interests of parts of society, that would be practically infeasible or that would otherwise be very hard to accept. Narrowing down the available courses of action ensures that the processes of formal decision making and law making are not entangled in a large number of impossible, unreasonable or irrelevant alternatives.

Secondly, macro deliberation can help us in cyclically revising our collective decisions (Benhabib 1996). Important issues can stay on the informal agenda of public discussion even when they are off the formal decision-making agenda. Thus, macro deliberation can serve to evaluate the effectiveness of our previous collective choices and return issues to the agenda if these choices produce unsatisfactory results, through a process that is analogous to the initial one of agenda setting.

Thirdly, a larger number of actors can participate than in any one micro deliberative meeting. Even the biggest sports stadia hold thousands, rather than hundreds of thousands or millions – no more than the population of a small town. And even if we filled a stadium with people, not all of them would be able to address a plenary session even if everyone had the opportunity to talk during small-group discussions. This kind of deliberative meeting is closer to the way in which Athenian democracy functioned, where many were present, but few actually acted (Ober 2008). In order to be effective, micro deliberation may need to be limited to an even smaller number of participants.

Macro deliberation, however, need not take place at the same time and in the same place. Indeed, it is often the by-product of other social activities (Cramer Walsh 2004; Perrin 2006), thereby reducing the cost of participation. Discussion is fragmented between multiple, overlapping public spheres (Fraser 1992; Benhabib 1996; Hendriks 2006). These consist of a multitude of groups and modes of communication. The important thing is that these groups are interlinked and able to communicate with each other, or even unable to completely ignore the communications of others. Individual citizens may be members of as many or as few groups as they wish.

Some of these discursive groups may contain people from different backgrounds, with a variety of views. However, many groups will consist of like-minded people and allow them to clarify and develop their beliefs in a safe environment. Thus, as well as a forum where views can be reasonably contested, the public sphere also accommodates the civil society associations that allow people to develop their political views in a supportive environment. This may be especially important for minorities and marginalized groups (Williams 1998; Young 2000).

Since macro deliberation is so widely dispersed, it raises problems for enforcing the standards of ideal theory. We would expect that both macro and micro deliberation are guided by norms of respect, other-regardingness, tolerance and civility, since these are defining characteristics of deliberative discussions. Nevertheless, equality and inclusion will be much harder to guarantee than in micro deliberation. Participating in the public sphere is much more difficult for those on the margins of society. It is also more likely that self-regarding or plebiscitary (Chambers 2004; see Chapter 5) discourse will persist.

The relation of micro deliberation to macro deliberation

The macro and micro models of deliberation are two related but very different expressions of the deliberative ideal. They each have their strengths and weaknesses. Normative standards can be more reliably secured in the case of micro deliberation. However, it is macro deliberation that transforms the nature of democratic decision making by allowing for a broad and inclusive debate in the public sphere. It is therefore important to ask what the relationship of these two models of deliberation is and should be in a well-functioning deliberative democracy.

Firstly, micro deliberation can play an important role in fostering macro deliberation. In a truly deliberative democracy, deliberation is not confined to small, micro settings, but instead permeates the political public sphere. However, the public sphere currently rarely reflects the normative standards of ideal deliberation and citizens are said to suffer from a considerable degree of political apathy. Micro deliberation can introduce them to debate along ideal normative standards, build a sense of civic duty and contribute to increased trust towards and engagement with the political system.

Secondly, micro deliberation can be a forum for decision making, while macro deliberation can serve agenda-setting and publicity functions. Discussion in the wider public sphere will at some stage have to be translated into legally binding collective decisions. There is no aspect of macro deliberation itself that can perform this function. Micro deliberation is much more suitable for this task, as it is most likely to function well if the topic of deliberation is well-defined and it is able to produce a unique decision either through consensual agreement or voting.

Of course, as we will see below, these two models of deliberation can also be integrated within a wider deliberative framework that includes elections, voting and bargaining. Thus the decisions of micro deliberative procedures can still be subject to a referendum, thereby ensuring legitimacy.

This follows the pattern that Habermas (1996a) has set out in his theory of *two-track deliberation*. The informal deliberative sphere serves as the background from which normative values, preferences and attitudes emerge and where they are discovered. This stage of deliberation is not aimed at decision making and is not organized or regulated. The formal deliberative sphere, on the other hand, consists of political actors and institutions. It is here that the political impulses of society are formally justified and are converted into law through formalized decision-making procedures. These two spheres are connected through elections, a mechanism that ensures that the norms and preferences of the wider and weaker public sphere are translated into the political sphere. 'This is a two-track model in which the informal public spheres are "contexts of discovery" and the formal, public spheres are "contexts of justification"' (Squires 2002, p.138).

Micro deliberation can also be of great use in giving a voice to those on the margins of society in the democratic system. This can be a direct result of deliberation, if recommendations and decisions form the basis of actual policy or if the results of the event are more widely publicized, and in indirect ways if micro deliberation increases people's confidence, ability and opportunity to participate in macro deliberative processes.

A major new development in contemporary democratic theory is the emergence of theories that integrate deliberative democracy with other modes of democratic decision making (Saward 2003; Parkinson 2003, 2006). These models of democracy incorporate micro and macro deliberation along with other forms of political events, such as voting or bargaining at appropriate phases of the decision-making process. Thus, none of these mechanisms are correct or right in themselves. Their appropriateness is instead determined by the circumstances under which they are used.

However this approach is different from the theory of deliberative democracy in one crucial respect. While deliberative democrats acknowledge that other forms of decision mechanisms, such as voting or bargaining, need to continue to exist alongside reasoned debate (see Chapter 5), they assert that deliberative debate is normatively more legitimate than these other methods and needs to take centre stage in the democratic decision-making process. Thus, the main aim of democratic theory is not to work out a sequencing of decision-making mechanisms that maximizes normative values, but instead it is to promote deliberation as the defining element of democracy.

Yet even deliberative democrats need to give attention to how deliberation can be integrated in a democratic polity. Especially in the case of macro deliberation, it becomes clear that it is hard to separate from other forms of political action. Much of the time these will not only coexist with, but also be intermingled with each other. Protests may trigger deliberation (Young 2001; Gutmann and Thompson 1996), but they may also have some deliberative content themselves. Thus, much of the time we may be dealing with hybrid forms of political action that are much harder to hold to the normative standards set out in the ideal theory. Deliberation will not only exist side by side with, but will be intermixed with strategic action, protest and bargaining.

Empirical Theory

It was not long before the theory of deliberative democracy took an empirical turn. This consisted both of theories of how the ideals of deliberative democracy could be implemented practically and of studies of deliberative and quasi-deliberative practices.

Many proposals have been put forward for introducing new, deliberative institutions into current democratic states. The most well-known of these are the deliberative polls developed by James Fishkin (Fishkin 1991, 2009; Ackermann and Fishkin 2004). According to the Center for Deliberative Democracy, 'the polling process reveals the conclusions the public would reach, if people had opportunity to become more informed and more engaged by the issues' (Center for Deliberative Democracy 2012a).

Deliberative polls have already become a reality. They have been held in many countries over diverse issues, such as the future of electric utilities in Texas, the future of the monarchy in Australia or discrimination against the Roma in Hungary and Bulgaria. Even the Chinese Communist Party has sanctioned some deliberative experiments (He and Leib 2006). One of the most recent polls was organized between citizens of different European Union member states and was conducted with the help of translators (Center for Deliberative Democracy 2012b).

Deliberative polls usually take place over a weekend. Before the start of the deliberative poll participants receive a pack of articles featuring balanced information for them to read through. This enables them to start deliberating with a basic understanding of the facts surrounding the issue at stake. Time over the weekend is divided between small-group discussions and larger expert panel sessions. The latter allow deliberators to address their questions directly to expert witnesses, stakeholders and politicians. The attitudes and preferences of deliberators are polled before and after deliberation.

Ackermann and Fishkin (2004) argue that these polls could be expanded to national politics, where citizens could meet in small groups locally to deliberate about the choices they are about to make in national elections. Citizens would thus be exposed to views different from their own as well as new facts. Hence they would be able to make a more reasoned decision come election day, based on the judgement they have arrived at after deliberation. In their work they have applied this model to deliberative meetings before federal elections in the United States and even referendums about the European Union (Ackermann and Fishkin 2008).

Other plans for introducing more deliberative institutions include the idea of formal deliberation on controversial policies among citizens, organized along the same lines as jury duty (Leib 2004), and formal deliberation among representative groups of citizens that create a report on candidates before elections (Gastil 2000) that other citizens can use to help them make an informed decision on election day. What all these possible institutional models have in common is that they aim to introduce new forms of formal deliberative meetings that uphold the normative values of the theory of deliberative democracy in a setting that is easy to control and regulate.

Such a formal deliberative procedure has been used in British Columbia, Canada to prepare a recommendation for a new state-wide electoral system (Warren and Pearse 2008). A representative sample of residents was asked to participate in a series of deliberative meetings called the British Columbia Citizens' Assembly, where they discussed with the help of expert advisers the possibility of replacing the existing first-past-the-post, majority rule system. Their recommendation was then put to citizens of the state in a referendum. While the deliberative process was hailed as a success, the proposal was rejected in the referendum.

Other, smaller-scale deliberative forums have been in use in policy making for a long time. The most well-known of these include citizens' juries, planning cells in Germany, debates organized by America Speaks and the Kettering Foundation, and consensus conferences. All of these bring together ordinary people for shorter periods of micro deliberation. These forums are run by professional organizers on behalf mostly of local authorities and their content has only been subject to relatively limited academic attention.

Making democracies more deliberative does not only consist of championing a top-down approach of introducing new institutions. There are also existing institutions which can be studied under the aegis of deliberative democracy and which could be modified or expanded to provide more opportunities for democratic deliberation.

Steiner *et al.* (2003, 2004) have carried out a detailed study of legislative deliberation in Germany, Switzerland, the United Kingdom and the United States. For this they developed a discourse quality index (DQI) which they used in textual analyses of legislative debates. The index measures whether legislators were able to state their arguments without interruptions, the level and content of justifications offered, the respect legislators showed towards other groups and other arguments and the extent to which political discourse aimed at building a consensus. While it may be a relatively rough tool, DQI enabled Steiner *et al.* to evaluate a large number of legislative debates in different types of democracies (parliamentary, presidential, majoritarian and consociational) and build up an overall picture of how institutional features affect the quality of discourse.

They found the largest differences concerned the level of respect legislators displayed towards others. They hypothesized that the quality of discourse would be higher in consociational and presidential systems, where the number of veto players is large, in second chambers, when the debates were not public and when issues under discussion were not polarized. The strongest evidence was in favour of consociational systems, veto players, second chambers and non-public arenas. The difference between different kinds of systems was in any case relatively small. As the authors emphasize, these systems are not worlds apart from each other. However, they argue that subtle differences can change the culture of political debates in the longer term.

Bryan (2004) has carried out a longitudinal study of New England town hall meetings, based on data he has gathered over a period of thirty years. While the project was conceived long before the deliberative turn in democratic theory and was primarily inspired by participatory theories of democracy, its results are no less relevant to the theory of deliberative democracy. Other community groups have also been examined from a deliberative perspective. Fung (2004) has studied deliberation on school boards and community police meetings. Studies of deliberative and quasi-deliberative processes have been carried out by numerous doctoral students, yet their results are not widely publicized.

The participatory budgeting procedure first introduced in Porto Alegre, Brazil, has been seen as an important testing ground for mass democratic deliberation (Gret and Sintomer 2005). Uniquely, this process allows participatory neighbourhood forums and special councillors selected from these forums to define municipal spending priorities. Rates of participation have been consistently high and despite shortcomings, there is evidence of genuine democratic deliberation.

Not all of these studies interpret democratic deliberation in the same way. Indeed as deliberative democracy has become a catch-all phrase, some of them seem to apply the concept to situations which are barely deliberative (Thompson 2008). However it is still this growing corpus of work that allows us most clearly to evaluate and refine the theory of deliberative democracy.

Main Lines of Critique

The theory of deliberative democracy is not without its critics. Some of the main lines of criticism emerged soon after the deliberative turn and have led to a significant refinement and, in some instances, a redefinition of the theory. While I highlight a few of these criticisms here, they will be discussed in much greater detail in the coming chapters.

Difference democrats (Young 1996, 2000; Benhabib 1996; Sanders 1997) focus on reducing the elitist connotations of democratic deliberation. Thus Young (1996, 2000) argued that this type of deliberation should not aim at academic rigour that could disadvantage those who were not used to this style of discourse. This could lead to inequality and exclusion, despite the stated objections of deliberative democrats. Instead, Young championed the idea of *communicative democracy* that embraces more forms of communication beyond formal debate and logical reasoning (more about this in Chapter 3). In particular, she discusses the importance of greeting, rhetoric and storytelling for inclusive dialogue. These aspects of communication not only break the hegemony of formal debate during deliberation, but also introduce a relational element into it. They are aimed at acknowledging others and establishing relationships with them (greeting), at persuading others (rhetoric) and at communicating a personal perspective (storytelling).

Others have argued that deliberative democracy makes cognitive demands that are too challenging for average citizens distracted by the demands of day-to-day life (Pincione and Tesón 2006; Lupia 2002). According to Hibbing and Theiss-Morse (2002), citizens want a well-functioning polity where their participation is limited to a minimum, hence they are unlikely to be motivated to participate in deliberative debates. Sunstein (2003), who is nevertheless a supporter of deliberative democracy, has pointed out that people will be swayed by things other than reason, will bow to peer pressure and jump on bandwagons (see Chapter 4). For these theorists, the role of emotion and rhetoric in reasoned deliberation is a more ambiguous one. Thus the outcome of deliberative debate will not always be better than individually made decisions would have been.

Particularly interesting are the cognitive weaknesses in decision making that arise from the fact that deliberation is undertaken by a *group*. Apart from peer pressure, conformity, groupthink and bandwagon effects, it is worth noting the possibility of group polarization (Sunstein 2003). If a group of people in favour of a policy gets together to deliberate, the initial beliefs and preferences of each member of that group are likely to get stronger. Discussions with like-minded individuals present us with more arguments for our initial position, without any real challenges to it, and also confirm the social acceptability of our position. While these effects comprise cognitive weaknesses, in themselves they are value-neutral. If the initial beliefs of group members were correct, there is no harm in confirming them. However, this is not meant to be the role of democratic deliberation and it therefore presents a normative problem even under the most benign circumstances.

The motivation of individuals to participate in inclusive, equal, reasoned and, most importantly, *other-regarding* debate can also be questioned. Even if citizens are willing to participate in deliberation, it is open to debate whether they will be willing to lay their selfish preferences and particular interests aside.

Some of these criticisms remain unanswered and I will take them up in the chapters that follow. Whatever the normative values of deliberative democracy, most of these highlight that in the real world there are likely to be significant deviations from the ideal model of deliberation. Furthermore, some of these criticisms mask an underlying concern with a conception of democracy that struggles to reconcile a demand for high standards with wide inclusion and a requirement of costly civic participation.

Plan of the Book

The aim of this book is to critically assess the components of deliberative democracy. In order to evaluate the theory, it will be contrasted with other alternatives throughout, most commonly with current liberal democratic models of democracy, which deliberative democrats aim to critique in theory and change in practice.

This will serve two purposes. First, in Chapters 2–5, I will develop a framework of values against which actual deliberative processes can be evaluated. The application of this will be illustrated in Chapters 6–7. Second, the primary purpose of my analysis is to provide a comprehensive review of the theory of deliberative democracy that allows us to identify its key strengths and weaknesses and to chart the direction in which contemporary democratic theory ought to move forward.

Chapter 2 will develop some of the theoretical ideas behind deliberation and address some of the fundamental questions about deliberation, such as when, where and why we should deliberate. The next three chapters provide the most crucial analysis in the book by evaluating the various normative values associated with the theory of deliberative democracy. Chapter 3 focuses on the value that reason can provide for democratic decision making and the ways in which deliberative democracy can arrive at epistemically good outcomes. Chapter 4 focuses on two of the most crucial values of any democratic theory: equality and inclusion. The theory of deliberative democracy does a good job of focusing on these two values, but does it offer viable ways of increasing equality and inclusion in democracies? Chapter 5 addresses the way in which deliberative democracies can deliver decisions and whether it is possible to integrate them coherently with other decision-making processes, such as voting or bargaining. Chapters 6 and 7 address the question of adopting better deliberative practices in current democracies. Chapter 7, in particular, offers an overview of some of the main ways this has been attempted so far. To conclude, Chapter 8 will offer an assessment of the theory of deliberative democracy as a whole as well as some thoughts on the ways in which democratic theory may develop in the future.

2
Deliberation in Detail

Now that we have a basic idea of what deliberative democracy is, it is time to unpack the concept in a bit more detail. What does it entail on the practical level? What purpose could it serve, where would it take place and who would participate? And what are the theoretical antecedents of the turn to deliberative democracy?

I will start this chapter with the theoretical questions. One of the core issues for democratic theorists is how the *legitimacy* of political decisions and decision-making processes can be increased. These aspects of democratic deliberation were addressed by two of the great political philosophers of the second half of the twentieth century: John Rawls and Jürgen Habermas. Their theoretical approaches are very different from each other, yet both point to the importance of deliberation. Examining why they do so can help us to develop a strong theoretical underpinning for our theory of deliberative democracy. This is important for any non-ideal or applied theory of politics; as they straddle grand theories of justice and legitimacy and empirical political science the temptation is always to focus on one of these aspects at the expense of the other.

The bulk of this chapter will be spent looking at categories which allow us to systematically explore deliberative democracy: the value of deliberation, its aims, topics suitable to it, and its location. Finally I will address some of the problems that these raise for the way in which we try to conceptualize democratic deliberation. These questions fall somewhere between the abstract theory and the practical application of democracy. Yet even though at times they may feel like a laundry list of problems to think about, they are no less important in developing a well-grounded theory. In political theory, after all, there is no such thing as 'just a definition', as it is more often than not the definitions that we end up arguing about.

Rawls and Habermas

In order to fully understand the theory of deliberative democracy, it is worth outlining its foundations in political theory. Deliberative democracy has been endorsed by the two most influential political theorists of the late twentieth century, Rawls and Habermas, despite the fact that their work falls under two very different schools in modern political theory. Rawls, a Kantian, is the most influential figure in contemporary Anglo-Saxon liberal political philosophy. Habermas, on the other hand, is a continental philosopher who emerged out of the Frankfurt school of critical theory. Not surprisingly, their approaches to the theory of deliberative democracy are also different.

Rawls turned to the possibility of a stable agreement over collective problems in a deeply pluralistic society in his later work, primarily in *Political Liberalism* (1993). In such societies people follow a number of different comprehensive doctrines or worldviews that determine their conception of the good. Such comprehensive doctrines can be liberal, religious, pacifist or environmentalist. Thus, people enter the political arena with different value systems that need to be negotiated if a stable decision is to be made. This can be achieved through what Rawls terms overlapping consensus. An overlapping consensus can be formed between people if all can accept a law or policy on the basis of their own competing reasonable comprehensive doctrines. This acceptance may at first be a *modus vivendi*, but is likely to evolve in the long term into a more genuine shared agreement.

This process takes place in the sphere of public reason. While there is no space here to provide a detailed definition of Rawls's theory of justice, it is important for our purpose to see how the idea of public reason fits into his work. The legitimacy of collective decision making under conditions of reasonable pluralism is grounded in the concept of *public reason*. For Rawls, legitimacy is '[t]o live politically with others in the light of reasons all might reasonably be expected to endorse' (1997: 116).

Public reason is public because (i) it is formulated by the public; (ii) its subject is the good of the public and matters of fundamental justice; and (iii) its nature and content are public (Rawls 1993, 1997). For Rawls, decisions about constitutional essentials need to be arrived at through the use of public reason. In his theory of justice as fairness, both the basic structure of society and the fundamentals of public reason are defined in the original position.

Public reason is characterized by *reciprocity*. As reasonable and rational members of a political community who recognize that citizens hold a diversity of reasonable views on the good, citizens should be ready to explain their positions in terms which are comprehensible and which they could expect others to also reasonably endorse. Thus reasons should not appeal only to those who hold the same comprehensive doctrines as we do, but to citizens of all worldviews. Thus through reciprocity, public reason ensures that political decisions are justifiable to all citizens. This need not mean that citizens can never refer to their comprehensive doctrines in public. Rawls takes an inclusive view of public reason that allows citizens to present the basis of their political values, provided they do so in a way that strengthens public reason (Rawls 1997: 119).

Cohen (1989/1997) unpacks Rawls's notion of public reason and bases on it an ideal theory of deliberative democracy and the conditions that enable it to thrive. According to his account, five main features are necessary for the existence of deliberative democracy. First, it is an ongoing and independent association and its members expect it to continue into the indefinite future. Second, members of this free association share a commitment that 'free deliberation among equals is the basis of legitimacy' (1997: 72). Third, their association is free and pluralistic and members are not required to subscribe to a common belief structure. Fourth, the connection between deliberation and outcomes should be evident to members of the group. Finally, members recognize appropriate deliberative capabilities in each other. This echoes Rawls's definition of public reason.

These five features set the background conditions under which proper public deliberation can operate. The ideal deliberative procedure itself is then characterized by four key features:

1. *Freedom.* Members of a deliberative democracy are bound only by the results of their own deliberation, and the fact that decisions are arrived at through deliberation is a sufficient reason to comply with them. Thus, only deliberative collective decisions have legitimate coercive power.

2. *Reason.* The results of deliberation depend only on the reasons members of the group present for making, defending or opposing a proposal. Thus it is the power of the best argument that works

in deliberation, rather than any other forms of power. Thus collective choices between a pluralistic group of individuals is made in a 'deliberative way' (p. 74), with the expectation that decisions are based on reason and a commitment to bringing about legitimate decisions based on deliberative principles.
3. *Equality*. Members of a deliberative democracy are both formally and substantively equal.
4. *Consensus*. The aim of ideal deliberation is to arrive at a consensus. In the absence of a consensus, decisions may be made through voting; however, the method of decision making is primarily deliberative and there is a strong commitment on the part of deliberators to make a consensual decision constrained by the condition of plurality.

Cohen's definition of deliberative democracy has been influential as the basis of the ideal liberal conception of the theory. Deliberative democrats have built on these abstract theoretical bases to develop a model of democracy that can address the shortcomings of liberal democracies in both theory and practice and recapture the essence of democratic politics.

Gutmann and Thompson (1996, 2004) claim to develop a mid-level theory of deliberative democracy that focuses neither on the legitimacy of ideal deliberation, nor on the development of new deliberative institutions, but on the legitimacy of everyday democratic processes (1996: p. 40). They follow a liberal, Rawlsian path that lays great emphasis on reasonableness and reciprocity. They examine how these values apply to decision making on concrete policy issues such as healthcare and education. Theirs is one of the first detailed and comprehensive articulations of a theory of deliberative democracy.

Habermas's theory of democracy has grown out of his work on speech act and discourse theory (1996a, b; Bohman and Rehg 1997), philosophical theories of how we use language to communicate and to shape the world around us. He has developed an influential inter-subjective theory of rationality, which he terms *communicative rationality*. Communicatively rational actors are able to share knowledge with each other in order to arrive at mutual understanding. Such communicative action contrasts with strategic action. Strategic actors are concerned with achieving their goals, rather than sharing and arriving at reasonable goals with others. In order to do this they need to offer valid reasons to each other that can then be further questioned and elucidated. Thus the entire process of language and discourse is driven by the desire to communicate content and have that content accepted by others.

For Habermas, ideal discourse takes place in an ideal speech situation. But the characteristics of this situation are by no means reified. First, everyone able to make relevant contributions should be included. Second, participants have equal voice in the debate. Third, participants are free to speak honestly, without internal or external deception or constraints. Finally, the process must be free of coercion. Discourse in such a situation will not only be communicatively rational, but it will also give power to the best argument.

It is this abstract work on speech act theory that then prompts Habermas to argue for a deliberative form of democracy in *Between Facts and Norms* (1996). He develops a model of law and politics that relies on proper discourse for its legitimacy. He conceptualizes deliberative democracy as a two-track model. Discourse in the public sphere can only be translated into valid laws through the work of an elected, discursive legislature. While this model remains abstract in nature, Habermas's work, especially his detailed articulation of discourse theory (see Chapter 3) has been a crucial influence on the theory of deliberative democracy and Dryzek (2000) has developed his model of *discursive democracy* more along Habermasian than Rawlsian lines.

Justifications of Democracy

The theories of Rawls and Habermas offer clear normative underpinnings for the theory of deliberative democracy. These theories are most clearly applied to democratic theory when we try to justify a form of democracy, that is, to argue that it is normatively valuable and legitimate.

Much of the normative discussion in this book will ask why deliberative democracy is valuable and, even more importantly, why it is better than other forms of democracy. Thus we need to define the grounds upon which we can justify democracy as a valuable procedure. This is not only important from a strictly theoretical point of view. There is also a more pragmatic question that we can answer in this way: why should citizens whose preferences did not prevail in the decision-making process accept the final outcome? Throughout we

have to keep in mind that we are not primarily contrasting deliberative democracy with non-democratic forms of government, but rather
with other models of democracy.

There are two main ways in which we can argue for the value of a
collective decision-making procedure: based on the characteristics of
the procedure itself and based on its outcome.

Procedural or intrinsic justifications appeal to the values inherent
in the process itself, such as equality, inclusion or self-determination.
These are not concerned with the outcomes of the procedure, but
with the way in which we can describe the procedure itself.

Democracy in general has very strong procedural justifications.
One of its core values is, after all, *political equality* (Beitz 1989; Dahl
1989; Dworkin 1987), which also manifests itself in the form of 'one
person, one vote'. Dahl defines democracy – or polyarchy, as he calls it
– in such procedural terms; government decisions are made by officials
elected in free and fair elections under universal suffrage, citizens have
a right to run for office, a right to freedom of expression, a right to
access alternative sources of information and a right to associational
autonomy (Dahl 1989: 221). The definition of deliberative democracy I have given in Chapter 1 is couched in such procedural terms: an
equal, inclusive, reasoned and other-regarding process aimed at solving collective problems.

The above discussion has already revealed that outcome-based or
instrumental justifications are concerned with the results of the procedure. We may want to argue that deliberative democracy is valuable
because it produces just outcomes, results in high levels of welfare or
it is good at identifying the best solution to problems (see Chapter 3).
Thus we are interested in the decision-making procedure primarily as
an *instrument* of bringing desired results about.

There are numerous examples of such instrumental justifications.
The welfarist argument states that democracy might result in higher
levels of welfare than other forms of political decision making. There
is a long-standing argument that democratic countries are less likely
to engage in war with one another (Ray 1998). Sen (1982) has argued
that democratic countries are much less likely to suffer famines. A
particularly relevant argument is that deliberative democracy might
lead to higher levels of social cohesion, more civic involvement and
citizens who are more knowledgeable about political issues.

The most common outcome-based justification of democracy is
the epistemic justification that argues that democracy is better at

tracking the truth or arrives at better decisions than other forms of collective decision making. Epistemic justifications are quite common for primarily electoral forms of democracy, but are also relevant for deliberative democracy (Chappell 2011). The theory's focus on the power of the best argument makes it clear that deliberation is not only valuable as a procedure itself, but will also tip the political balance in favour of good decisions. Chapter 3 will examine this idea in detail.

Both epistemic and procedural justifications can play an important role in establishing the legitimacy of a decision-making procedure. Procedural justifications appeal to fewer controversial standards of evaluation. They do not appeal to notions of correctness or goodness over which there may be great scope for reasonable disagreements. Yet we do not only care about the fairness of our decision-making procedures and it would not be difficult to argue for change if a decision-making procedure consistently produced bad outcomes. Ultimately, procedural and outcome-based justifications for democracy are unlikely to exist independently of each other (Chappell 2011), therefore I will give both of them equal weight in my analysis of the theory of deliberative democracy.

Meaning and Understanding

Whether we justify democracy procedurally or based on the outcomes it produces, the aim of legitimate collective decisions is to resolve conflicts and to make decisions over issues which have to be decided collectively due to their very nature. Policies on public health-care, clean air or policing can never be decided by each individual in a community in isolation, as they require the solution of coordination problems and the application of moral and ethical principles about the way a just society should function.

Meaningful politics requires that sufficient differences should exist between groups to make getting involved in politics worthwhile. If all members of a community unanimously agree about a decision without deliberation, there are no incentives for individuals to take part in politics. The fact that different individuals and groups hold different sets of values or rank the same values differently means that the outcomes of politics matter to citizens. Hibbing and Theiss-Morse (2002) argue that the reason most citizens are not interested in participating in politics is that they overestimate the extent of consensus in society. Thus heterogeneity of beliefs and a realization that this heterogeneity exists play a crucial role in motivating individuals to participate in politics.

Of course not all levels of heterogeneity are beneficial. Sometimes cleavages can be so deep that different groups find it impossible to talk to each other. This situation can lead to catastrophic consequences, such as civil war or genocide. In these cases it is more feasible to start out by developing a relationship between the two communities through more group interest-focused and less deliberative means. These procedures could then be made more deliberative in the future.

So what kind of homogeneity does successful deliberation require? At the very minimum, participants need to be able to communicate with each other without difficulties. This presupposes that members of a society share a common language, even if in some cases, such as that of Canada, Switzerland or India, citizens in different regions speak different languages. While language itself may not pose a barrier for deliberation, citizens also need to possess a shared understanding of the world around them, in terms of understanding how the political system works and understanding the key values of democratic societies, such as freedom of expression. This is necessary in order to fulfil the condition of reciprocity in deliberation, whereby participants appeal to shared reasons (Gutmann and Thompson 1996). If a significant section of a population is not committed to upholding the values of democracy, then they are unlikely to be willing to participate in deliberation. There is evidence that acceptance of such values is generally common in societies, even though the extent to which they are embraced might differ across individuals or groups (Dryzek and Braithwaite 2000). But even in well established democracies there will be some citizens who do not seek to uphold democracy or who do not subscribe to otherwise commonly shared notions of equality or justice. These groups can pose special problems for deliberative democracy, as they would find it difficult, if not impossible, to participate in deliberation effectively.

Even when citizens of a country nominally share common values, it could be difficult to evaluate whether they interpret those values in the same way. This could result from the shorthand use of terms such as 'equality', which could mean both equality of opportunity and equality of outcome. Or it could be the result of different interpretations of

the same term, such as 'freedom of speech', which some might interpret as limitless, while others would exclude crudely hateful or
discriminatory speech. In these cases citizens may end up talking past
each other, even if deliberation does take place. Therefore the depth
of deliberation matters. Either fundamental values need to be probed
and clarified or deliberation has to be very clearly limited to a few
policies or issues at a time, where decisions are made about the means
of achieving an end, rather than the end itself.

Dryzek and Braithwaite (2000) studied different sets of values
among the Australian electorate and arrived at a four-fold division of
value conflicts. First, two distinct, but most likely overlapping value
sets could face each other. This is the case in traditional left–right politics. Second, a group with a set of values might be faced with a group
which held no values and was cynical about them. This could be the
case when citizens become disaffected with the political and the social
system. The authors argue that in these two cases meaningful deliberation is possible, either when reflection is inspired between two sets of
values or when those with positive values try to bring the valueless
along with them. The third and fourth cases, however, are not
amenable to deliberative procedures. In the third case a group defines
itself in opposition to another group's values without developing a
coherent value set itself. This can lead to a dogmatic definition of their
positions, which deliberation is unlikely to change, as whatever one
party says, the others will say just the opposite in order to contradict
them. In the fourth and final case a group's values are rejected entirely
by another group. Dryzek and Braithwaite find no evidence for this
case in their study. However, there is certainly some alarming evidence
indicating that there are some who reject liberal values more or less
completely, albeit these individuals are in a small minority. An example of such rejection of values can be witnessed in some of the slogans
that protests against the infamous Danish Mohammed cartoons –
that have not only depicted the prophet (this is not allowed under the
rules of Islam) but have made him a character in funny cartoons – have
produced. These slogans, one of which was 'Freedom go to hell', deny
the right to free speech and as such fundamentally oppose Western
liberal values. It is ironic that it was the values which they denounce
that allowed them to publicize their renunciation in the first place.

Thus deliberative politics in particular and democratic politics in
general rely on getting the balance between homogeneity and heterogeneity right. A society needs to be homogeneous enough to allow its

members to understand each other and be able to solve problems peacefully and cooperatively. At the same time politics requires a tension between the interests of different groups, which needs to be resolved. Without this tension politics loses its meaning and can be replaced by mere bureaucracy. The danger that deliberation accentuates is that many groups in a pluralistic society talk past each other. This could lead to a general lack of understanding, which could undermine the effectiveness of deliberative discourse.

Having established the basis on which the theory of deliberative democracy rests, the rest of this chapter will be devoted to developing some broad characterizations within which we can think of deliberative democracy: the various purposes democratic deliberation can serve, the topics most suitable to deliberation, the possibility of global deliberation and the link between deliberation and representation.

The Purpose of Deliberative Meetings

Deliberation can serve a number of vital functions beyond decision making. I will discuss four of these here: agenda setting, exploration, recommendation and preference formation. Importantly, each of these works towards enhancing the legitimacy of democratic decision-making processes.

As we have seen above, agenda setting is primarily applicable to macro deliberation, which plays a crucial role in identifying the most salient issues and acceptable solutions to them. However, micro deliberation can also have an agenda-setting role if a group is called together in order to name the problems that they would like to see solutions developed for. One of the first stages in the participatory budgeting procedure in Porto Alegre, Brazil, takes the form of neighbourhood and topical assemblies that local residents and residents' associations attend in order to decide which municipal problems the city administration should prioritize over the next year (Gret and Sintomer 2005; covered in greater detail in Chapter 7). Similarly, the organizers of neighbourhood deliberation in Groningen, the Netherlands, asked local residents to decide which local day-to-day infrastructural problems ought to be tackled by the local authority (University of Groningen 2010). While such deliberation makes decisions about the issues which are most important, it leaves the development of solutions and implementation to other bodies.

The primary purpose of a deliberative meeting is exploratory if its aim is to gain a better understanding of an issue, common views on it and possible solutions to it. Such exploratory deliberation places more importance on finding out about the differences and common-alities of people's views and the complexities of the issue than on arriving at a solution. This can be useful in the early stages of collec-tive decision making, when we need to find out how people view an issue, what the most relevant issue dimensions are for decision making and what the main points of conflict are between different members of a community. It can also be useful for bringing together people with very different experiences and points of view and allow-ing them to gain a better understanding of why others may disagree with them. This has been the purpose of race relations forums that have brought together white and African-American residents of the same city, so members of both groups could learn about each other's life experiences and race-specific problems (Chambers 2004). This can also be a useful approach for intractable moral problems where only one path can be chosen to the detriment of the other. Thus, for example, we can bring together pro-life and pro-choice activists not with the aim that one side will persuade the other to abandon their position, but with the aim that both sides will learn more about the reasons why others hold their views and learn to respect them more in the process – an important aspect of life in a democratic society.

Deliberation can also serve to deliver recommendations. This is not only true for expert committees or a micro deliberative group of citizens making recommendations to an executive or a legislature. The purpose of numerous micro deliberative projects has been just this. In the UK a citizen jury has delivered recommendations on the use of nanotechnology to the executive and citizens' juries have been used to help the National Health Service in making decisions.

More than one micro deliberative event has been organized with the aim of arriving at a recommendation on an important issue provided by ordinary, albeit very well-informed, voters to other ordinary voters. The participants of the British Columbia Citizens' Assembly (Warren and Pearse 2008) were selected through random sampling among citizens of that state and their conclusions formed the basis on which a referendum was held on voting reform. Thus they invested their time and other resources as part of their civic duty to tell the other residents of their state how their electoral system could best be reformed. Gastil (2000) argues for holding micro deliberative events discussing issues and candidates among a random sample of citizens and publicizing the results before election day. Fishkin *et al.* (2002; see also Farrar *et al.* 2010) have organized deliberative polls around a British national election and the referendum in Australia on the continuation of the monarchy in order to discover and publicize what arguments and choices well-informed citizens would make.

Preference formation is meant to be an integral part of all deliberative processes. Through an open-minded exchange of arguments and sincerely paying attention to the viewpoints of others, as well as through learning new facts, deliberators are expected to change their beliefs or preferences, or establish their preferences over an issue if previously they had no settled preference. However, some instances of deliberation prioritize such preference formation and transformation. The purpose of 'deliberation day' (Ackermann and Fishkin 2004) would be to enable citizens to vote on election day on the basis of considered and well-informed preferences. Similarly, much of public sphere deliberation serves to inform people about new and contentious issues to enable them to form their own beliefs and preferences.

The Topic of Deliberation

The most obvious way we can ascertain what subjects are suitable for deliberation is by looking at the context in which it takes place. The design of a local library might be a perfectly suitable topic for local town hall meetings (Karpowitz and Mansbridge 2005), while it would be a waste of time at the national level. Whether Australia should be a constitutional monarchy can be debated at the national level (Fishkin *et al.* 2002), but it would make little sense to decide on this at the local town hall level. Of course which issues are discussed at each level also depends on the political organization of each country. Some countries are more centralized than others, which leave more decisions to be taken at the local level. But according to Habermas (1996b), increased deliberation will coincide with decentralization.

At its most ambitious, the purpose of micro deliberation among citizens is to make a decision. For such deliberative processes, a very specific issue with well-defined options to choose from is most suitable. Examples of these could include decisions on whether or not a road should be built through a forest (Goodin and Niemeyer 2003), decisions on healthcare budget priorities (Gutmann and Thompson 1996) and decisions on how a school should be run (Fung 2004). But not all topics are equally likely to lead to successful deliberation, as defined by the procedural values in the literature. While the context of deliberation can give us important guidelines as to the suitability of issues, it does not answer the question fully. We need to ask ourselves: whatever the setting is, what kind of question is deliberation most likely to be successful in answering? There are two criteria which are crucial for the success or failure of micro deliberation among citizens, issue complexity and issue salience.

The complexity of issues that can be discussed in a deliberative meeting between ordinary citizens is relatively limited. Issue complexity increases both with an increase in the knowledge necessary for making well-informed judgements and with the number of issue dimensions involved in making the decision. Citizens' juries have deliberated on some complex issues, such as the use of nanotechnology, but this can only be undertaken with the help of expert witnesses and at a level of complexity and understanding that reflects the abilities of the deliberative group. Thus, for technically complex problems citizens should only be required to understand the basic principles of the issues at stake to the extent that they will be able to make informed judgements about their social, economic and moral implications.

The more complex the issues, the more time is required to acquire the necessary knowledge to make informed judgements. Just as some technically complex legal cases are ruled on by judges rather than juries, some complex questions may be better left to expert, rather than citizen deliberation. The cognitive demands of such issues may make deliberation too costly for average citizens, in terms of both time and effort (Reykowski 2006; Hibbing and Theiss-Morse 2002).

The complexity of an issue is reduced if the options that deliberators can choose from are pre-determined and their number is limited. It can also be reduced if the problem does not have a significant moral dimension, as this is likely to lead to less, or at least less intense, disagreement. Complexity is also lessened if deliberators are already familiar with the issue at stake. Stakeholder groups may be able to deliberate on relatively complex matters more easily. As an example, parents of school-age children may be more aware of options for improving a school's performance than other citizens are. However, they may also have stronger beliefs and preferences already in place, which are then more difficult to change.

Thus deliberation is more likely to be successful if issues are not too complex. Fewer issue dimensions, a lower requirement for highly technical knowledge and a familiarity with the issues will reduce the time and effort required to come to a reasoned decision. However, no general rules exist that will always predict the success of deliberation; this will instead be highly context-sensitive.

Some authors have argued in the past that deliberation is only necessary in the case of highly significant events, such as constitution building. However, theorists have moved away from this view. For example, while Ackermann held this view in *We the People* (1991), he no longer does so in *Deliberation Day* (2004). But even *Deliberation Day* urges us to use public mass deliberation infrequently – only at times of elections. The reason for reducing the number of issues we deliberate on is usually a lack of resources, most notably time and motivation. Thus while deliberation may be successful for less salient issues, its cost will not necessarily be justified by the personal and collective benefits received from it.

Whether deliberation takes place on the local, national or global level, the number of instances in which this process can be used will be limited. One way of determining whether we should decide on an issue using formal deliberative meetings is by establishing whether there is a demand for them. If an issue is uncontroversial, then existing political arrangements, such as decisions reached by the legislature or the executive, can take care of it. The number of issues people will actually want to deliberate on will be limited, since much of the time citizens just want politicians to get on with governing without involving them (Hibbing and Theiss-Morse 2002). But there are also issues where there appears to be at least some public demand for more debate and consultation.

Where Should We Deliberate?

Deliberation can be implemented over many levels of government. At the national level some ideas for implementing deliberation encompass the whole population, either formally (Ackermann and Fishkin 2004; Leib 2004) or informally (Benhabib 1996). For other authors, national-level deliberation is focused on elected legislatures (Steiner *et al.* 2004) or specialist deliberative assemblies (Elstub 2008). But deliberation can also take place at the local level (Fung 2004), in town halls (Mansbridge 1980) or in consultative bodies made up of citizens (Baiocchi 2003; Souza 2001). Finally, deliberation is seen to be suitable for extending outside the nation-state, to a global level (Dryzek 2006).

Probably the most controversial of these is the idea of global deliberation. In a globalized world, opportunities exist for both international macro and micro deliberation. Micro deliberation could form part of the decision-making methods of international organizations as well as negotiations between nation states. As a result of globalization, macro deliberation is of necessity to some extent global. Information and opinions are exchanged between citizens of various countries – just think of the classrooms of many universities, – much of the world's population is increasingly globally mobile and media and telecommunications allow information and discourses to travel and spread across the world. Even demonstrations and protests can be global events nowadays, drawing participants from many countries.

As a result of globalization, political decisions increasingly have to be made about issues which are not only complex, but also straddle existing state boundaries. This challenges the legitimacy and decision-making capacity of classical nation states. Democratic deliberation, no longer centred around the state, could overcome this gap in legitimacy. Deliberation could also be crucial in increasing the legitimacy of supranational organizations, such as the European Union (Habermas 1996b; Ackermann and Fishkin 2008).

Dryzek (2006) argues that today's world is characterized by conflict between discourses, rather than conflict between rival states. Thus he constructs a discursive theory of contemporary conflict, while rejecting the theory of a clash of civilizations (Huntington 1996) or a realist model of international relations. Globalization, sustainable development, counter-terrorism or Islamic fundamentalism are all examples of such discourses. In today's world hegemonic discourses are questioned more and more, leading to the development of new discourses through reflexive modernization and stronger adherence to old ones through reflexive traditionalization.

Dryzek uses this framework to argue for international discursive democracy, a model of global politics where actors recognize the importance of rival discourses and aim to develop dialogue between groups. Engagement between discourses is assumed to lead to reconciliation or at least an easier coexistence between them, even in deeply divided societies.

Dryzek conceptualizes global deliberation as an ongoing, largely informal process that takes place within a network of international groups. Global civil society actors are more suited to this task than nation states and large international organizations, as they are more flexible and can introduce and use new discourses more freely. This model of global deliberation partly corresponds to the model of macro deliberation.

Global deliberation, however, often introduces distance and heterogeneity that can be a profound challenge for deliberation in the theoretical sense of the word. It is of course possible to communicate across the globe, but how much of this communication will be deliberative? And how could the normative standards of deliberation be secured in a global public sphere? At the global level, links between public sphere deliberation and actual decisions made by states and international organizations may be particularly difficult to secure, thereby negating any gains in legitimacy.

And even if politics on the global level may become more deliberative, this does not mean that it will become more democratic. More powerful or resource-rich states will still dominate international relations. Not all countries will be equally able to set global discourse, especially as more powerful countries also have a wider range of international actions available to them, such as the capability to start wars, and their own domestic politics will also have more negative and positive externalities that will affect the citizens of other countries

Furthermore, it will be well organized groups, whether they are NGOs, pressure and protest groups or even terrorist organizations, that are most able to shape the deliberative discourse to their own advantage. But these groups will not necessarily be representative of global discourse in general. They may receive high pay-offs from the issues they represent, such as those farmers who are even willing to set themselves alight at World Trade Organization meetings in protest against a lowering of tariffs, or they may have a special ideological commitment to a cause, as many committed anti-globalization protesters do. Groups with diffuse costs and benefits will find it much less easy to set up effective collective organizations. Even though nearly all humans are consumers of rice and as such they are far more numerous than those involved in farming rice, the benefits of participating for each individual are relatively low, while its costs are high and therefore it is likely that the minority rice farmers will be more successful activists than the majority consumers.

The poor and those who have limited access to new communication technologies, such as the Internet, will not be able to participate in global deliberation either, as they will not have access to it. This blatantly violates the principles of substantive equality and of inclusion. This problem could be overcome by strengthening international bodies, such as the United Nations, which then could make a claim to represent everyone (Young 2004). However, it is debatable how strong or legitimate this claim to representation can be without a complete global restructuring of power relations and resource distributions (Young 2004).

Thus, while there may exist a deliberative or discursive, rather than purely power-driven element in international politics, this will be neither fully deliberative nor fully democratic. Therefore, if we want to introduce deliberative *democracy*, it is much more fruitful to focus on national- and local-level deliberative processes.

Deliberation on the national level is the topic of some of the more ambitious projects on micro deliberative democracy, such as Ackermann and Fishkin's 'deliberation day' (2004). National deliberation, however, introduces problems of scope and representation (Parkinson 2003) that are not nearly as acute on the local level. Even if it were possible for all citizens to deliberate on national-level issues occasionally, such as on deliberation day, some form of representation would need to be adopted for most national-level decisions.

Deliberation on the local level, on the other hand, is often regarded as the most authentic form of deliberation. Most deliberative studies deal with local-level deliberation: town hall meetings (Karpowitz and Mansbridge 2005), school board meetings (Fung 2004), participatory budget procedures (Baiocchi 2003; Souza 2001).

Deliberation among citizens on local-level issues has many characteristics that are likely to make it successful. The issues discussed are relevant and close to individuals. They are clearly defined and tend to be relatively easy to understand. They are usually also practical in nature – for example, whether a new community centre should be built – rather than involving complex moral and ethical issues. Possible solutions to problems are also clearly identifiable. Deliberators often have a common interest that is stronger than it would be in the case of national deliberation. The results of the deliberative procedure are usually immediate, thus residents feel the direct benefits of participating. Deliberation can even have the beneficial effect of building up community cohesion.

Thus, deliberative democracy may be an ideal tool for solving local problems in a way that includes and mobilizes rather than alienates residents. Local-level deliberation allows for homogeneity and familiarity with each other which cannot be achieved on the national and global levels. Hence, to a large extent, local-level deliberation is closest to the ideal model.

It is also much more feasible to organize face-to-face deliberative meetings at a local level than it is at a national or regional one. But even in a relatively small town, problems of scope resurface, as it would not be possible to get all adult residents to participate simultaneously. Even if a town or city was small enough, so that all adult residents could fit into a stadium together, they would not be able to deliberate together, unless participants were divided into smaller groups.

If the theory of deliberative democracy is to fulfil its purpose of increasing the extent to which there is a *society-wide* increase in the exchange of reasons and a transformation of beliefs and preferences that will profoundly affect politics, this would need to take place both on the local level among ordinary citizens and on the national level among citizens, activists and politicians. Thus a complete model of deliberative democracy would need to combine micro and macro, local and national deliberation for a blueprint of an entirely deliberative polity.

Thus, we can say that the primary site of *democratic* deliberation will remain the nation state. But here, there is still significant work to be done on developing a model of deliberation that spans both national and local politics. Only in this way can we guarantee that a pervasive deliberative culture would have the opportunity to emerge. Of course such a deliberative system would not be easy to design, as it would have to balance and motivate deliberation on different levels against other forms of decision making, such as bargaining.

Deliberation and Representation

The discussion so far has shown that the practical scope for true face-to-face deliberation, especially on the national level, but even on the local level, is limited. A special problem is presented if we want to mix public sphere deliberation among all citizens with more formal micro deliberation among representatives. The problem is as follows. Citizens are usually thought to elect representatives in order to make sure that their preferences and interests receive proper weight in the legislative process. However, deliberation requires *preference change* and probably also *belief change* from deliberators. It is this transformative quality that is one of the key defining features of deliberative democracy. Yet, this transformation will only take place in the *representatives* and not in their *constituents*. We can take it as a reasonable demand of appropriately deliberate processes that they should be transparent and that representatives are required to make every effort to give reasons for their preferences, beliefs and decisions to those they represent. This, however, may not always be enough to convince their constituents that their choice was the right one. Thus we are faced with a fundamental paradox. On the one hand, representatives are required to represent their constituents faithfully. On the other hand, deliberators are required to be open to a transformation of beliefs and preferences. These two ideas need to be reconciled somehow in order for micro deliberation between representatives to be normatively legitimate.

There has not been a satisfactory answer to this paradox so far. To argue that representatives should attempt to justify the positions they reach through deliberation to constituents without taking further account of the views of the latter (Gutmann and Thompson 1996) is an unsatisfactory answer from the point of view of constituents. Therefore we must ask ourselves what model of representation deliberative democracy would imply and what accountability means in a deliberative context (Mansbridge 2003).

Most models of representation view the selection of representatives either as an evaluation of the promises of prospective policies candidates will carry out if elected or as a retrospective evaluation of candidates' past performance in office (Mansbridge 2003).

The idea that representatives are the delegates of their constituents is not new. According to this concept of representation, parties or candidates prepare manifestos or other statements as to their intentions during their time in office. Voters make their decisions about which candidate to elect based on these stated intentions. Once representatives are in office they are seen to possess a mandate to carry out these policies and are held accountable if they fail to do so. This is clearly an inappropriate model of representation for deliberative democracy. While representatives in truly deliberative processes may be able to promise their constituents to put forward certain arguments which are important to them during the debate, they cannot promise to push forward certain policies without being willing to change their position.

According to the second conception of representation, voters do not vote in elections based merely on the stated intentions of candidates. Rather, they evaluate the past performance of incumbents and use voting as an opportunity to 'throw the rascals out' and 'keep the good ones in'. Thus, voting is retrospective (Fiorina 1978, 1981). The electorate perceive the outcomes of politicians' actions in office, together with a random noise. If they believe that someone could do better than the incumbent, they get rid of him. This model of representation is reflected in politicians' efforts to keep themselves informed of their constituents' preferences through public opinion polls and focus groups. Again, this is not a suitable model of representation for deliberative democracy, as it constrains the actions of representatives during deliberation and would not allow for belief transformation if this did not correspond with the preferences of the electorate.

Neither of these models allows enough independence for deliberative representatives to participate in a fully deliberative assembly. There is, however, another model of representation that may be more applicable to the deliberative setting. The origins of this model lie in the idea that representatives are trustees, not delegates (Burke 1774/1999). Here representatives need to be given free rein to vote for policies which they perceive to be fit, as their constituents may not have as good an understanding of problems and as good an idea of the common good as they do. Representatives are seen as worthy individuals who can be trusted by their constituents to do the right thing. Early modern democracies approximated this model more closely than later ones (Manin 1997).

Jane Mansbridge (2003) calls a broader version of this model 'gyroscopic representation'. In this model constituents do not simply try to identify the candidate whose manifesto is closest to their preferences or who adhered to their wishes most closely while in office. Rather, voters try to identify the representative who is a 'good type', someone whose interests and judgements coincide with those of their constituents and who has sound principles. Fearon (1999) argues that voters often see elections in this light. They prefer principled candidates to ones who follow public opinion like a weathervane. What is necessary is what Mansbridge (2003: 521) calls 'deep predictability' – voters want to elect representatives whose actions and decisions they can predict based on their past behaviour, character and so on.

This seems to be a much more appropriate model for representation in a deliberative assembly. Thus, constituents will choose representatives who will behave during deliberation similarly to how they would themselves behave and whose preferences are transformed in the way that their preferences would be transformed. If they feel confident that their representatives are deeply predictable in this way, then they will trust their decisions more than they would otherwise.

Of course, even under this model of representation we would have to accept that constituents would sometimes find it difficult to understand why their representatives made certain decisions in the deliberative assembly. Here transparency and communication between constituents and representatives become supremely important. Thus, a layer of deliberation would need to exist between representatives and their constituency. Constituents must be able to communicate their concerns to the representative and representatives must justify their decisions to their constituents under deliberative conditions, particularly under conditions of reciprocity.

The second question is how citizens would be able to recognize good types. There is a large literature that argues that citizens use heuristic cues in choosing which candidate to elect (Grofman and Withers 1993). However, one could question whether this information is sufficient for citizens to identify which politicians would be able to represent them best in a deliberative procedure. Due to extensive media coverage, there is usually a great deal of information available about politicians in high-profile positions. Yet citizens may need to invest a lot of time into becoming sufficiently informed to make up their minds about the character of candidates. Shortcuts and soundbites are less costly sources, but could be misleading as they can be easily manipulated to present politicians in a better light. In the end no amount of information will compensate for not personally knowing a candidate, which is inevitable in large electorates.

A bigger problem is making sure that representatives' preferences are not transformed in a way that will harm their constituents' interests. After all, they are not identical to each other and therefore the representative may not be aware of all aspects of his constituents' beliefs and preferences. This highlights a fundamental tension between interests and deliberative belief transformation. In most cases it is the interests and beliefs of citizens that should be privileged by representatives, if they cannot go through an identical belief or preference change themselves. Otherwise the legitimacy and validity of democratic representation can be called into question by citizens. Thus, even if we employ a trustee model of representation, the initial paradox between representing specific constituents and deliberative transformation is still not fully resolved.

The Inclusion of Those Who Normally Do Not Have a Say in National Politics

A final issue that needs to be raised regarding the participants of deliberative democracy is the problem of those who are not traditionally included in politics. Here I am primarily thinking of those residents of a country who are not citizens, but this category could also include future generations, animals or the government and citizens of other countries that are affected by policies with significant externalities, such as pollution control. While I am not able to offer a solution for this problem here, the issue is worth highlighting, as it is much harder to exclude people from deliberative public discourse than it is to do so from voting or even formalized, micro deliberative processes.

The kind of stable liberal representative democracies that can be seen as good candidates for the introduction of deliberative democracy often have relatively large non-citizen immigrant populations. In the United Kingdom, 5.2 per cent of the population are foreign nationals (OECD 2007). These immigrants do not have the same political rights as other members of society. In European Union (EU) countries a hierarchy of residents has developed where citizens hold full political rights, citizens of other EU countries hold partial rights and other residents hold some residual rights (Cohen 1987). Furthermore, in the UK, due to an anachronism in electoral law dating back to 1918, nationals of Commonwealth countries are allowed to vote in the national election, while non-British immigrants from other countries are not.

Medium- and long-term residents are affected by political decisions just as much as full citizens are. The question is whether they should be excluded from deliberation just as they are excluded from voting or indeed whether it is possible to exclude them at all.

Under a macro model of deliberation non-citizens would also be able to participate, as there would be no formal way of excluding anyone from the public sphere. Under a micro model of deliberation it would be possible to exclude non-citizens, but one could argue that an intermediate stage of political rights should be developed where non-citizens could put forward their arguments and could serve the role of expert witnesses, but would not be able to vote on a final decision. Most likely, deliberation would ultimately be supplemented by voting (Goodin 2008), therefore it may be possible to include non-citizens in some formal deliberation, while leaving final decisions to citizens. This would allow non-citizens to have a voice and present their arguments about policies which would have significant effects on their lives. Yet the status of non-citizen immigrants raises a significant question as to where the line of deliberative inclusion should be drawn.

Conclusion

These first two chapters have established some important definitions and have allowed us to think of democratic deliberation in a more organized way. The stage is now set for starting to evaluate some of the procedural and epistemic claims made by deliberative democrats. I have defined deliberative democracy as decision making through reasoned, other-regarding, equal and inclusive debate. In Chapter 3 I will tackle the first part of that definition – reason and other-regardingness – while Chapter 4 will be concerned with equality and inclusion.

3

Deliberation, Reason and Rationality

In Chapter 1, I defined deliberative democracy as reasoned, other-regarding, equal and inclusive debate aimed at making collective decisions. In this chapter I will be concerned with the second half of this definition: the characteristics and benefits of other-regarding, reasoned deliberation.

There are two main ways in which we can argue for the value of democratic decision-making processes. Proceduralists do so based on the values embodied in the procedure itself. Outcome-based justifications, on the other hand, place the value of a procedure in the fact that it arrives at good outcomes. What makes the reasoned-based qualities of deliberation so interesting is that, as I will show in this chapter, they are important for both of these justifications.

But what are these reason-based qualities of democratic deliberation? Deliberation is reasoned inasmuch as it brings about *preference change* through *reciprocal* and *other-regarding* debate. The chapter will start by examining these three ideas, before outlining ways in which reasoned discussion can contribute to a procedural justification of deliberative democracy. But the most important contribution of reason is clearly to the epistemic justification of deliberative democracy, to which the majority of this chapter will be devoted.

Preference Change

One of the most significant points made by deliberative democrats is that we should expect citizens' preferences to change in the political forum. Some earlier models of democracy, especially ones that are based on rational or social choice theory, take preferences to be fixed. Each individual citizen enters the political arena with fully formed, rational preferences in place and the function of the political process is to aggregate these inputs into a collective output or policy choice. Minimalist conceptions of democracy (for example, Riker 1982) could also be accused of taking a non-cognitivist view of preferences and voting. Thus these theories do not require votes to be the product of a reflective process aimed at identifying the best decision, no matter how we define 'best'. Preferences are viewed as rational insofar as they fulfil a set of basic conditions that ensures that individuals do not hold contradictory positions, but minimal conceptions of democracy remain silent about the origin of those preferences or the extent to which they correspond to the actual interests of individuals.

The theory of deliberative democracy, on the other hand, assumes that the political process will contribute to shaping these preferences or inputs. This can happen in two ways. First, it is reasonable to suppose that citizens do not have fully formed preferences in place and do not know their own minds about each and every collective problem. Deliberation can thus have a function of preference formation, as citizens are required to articulate their preferences in the public forum as well as listen to the preferences of others and increase their factual knowledge. Second, these processes may also lead deliberators to change the preferences they already have in place, thereby inducing preference transformation. Theories of deliberative democracy shift the focus to the creation and transformation of preferences through reciprocal, reasoned discussion. Thus, 'the more collective decision-making processes approximate this [deliberative] model the more increases the presumption of their legitimacy and rationality' (Benhabib 1996: 69).

Reciprocity

One of the most important conditions for deliberation, endorsed across the entire literature on deliberative democracy, is that it should be characterized by reciprocity (Benhabib 1996; Gutmann and Thompson 1996; Fung 2004). Reciprocity requires participants (1) to justify their judgements and preferences in terms that are acceptable to other, reasonable individuals; and (2) to be willing to listen to arguments presented by others in a similarly publicly oriented way. Thus deliberative democracy makes use of the Rawlsian idea of public reason (Rawls 1993).

Deliberation increases the rationality and reasonableness of decisions by requiring deliberators to justify their judgements and preferences publicly. It increases its rationality, because deliberators will be more aware of what is in their own best interest as well as in the best interest of others. It increases reasonableness, as it increases the extent to which deliberative debates are based on shared norms, such as fairness. Reciprocity defines the kinds of reasons that are acceptable for such justifications. These reasons take into account that political deliberation will take place in pluralistic societies (Cohen 1996) where not all citizens share the same worldview. Worldviews or systems of beliefs are often termed comprehensive doctrines following Rawls. Any decision that can be justified publicly must be acceptable to all citizens, no matter what comprehensive doctrine they hold. This makes reciprocity not only a source of rationality, but also of legitimacy.

Reasons are acceptable first, if substantive moral reasoning appeals to premises which individuals could plausibly accept from the perspective of their particular comprehensive doctrine, even if they do not in fact do so, and second, if they appeal to premises which rely on empirical evidence that can be tested according to reliable methods of enquiry (Gutmann and Thompson 1996: 56).

Reciprocity is not as demanding as it may appear at first sight. It is less demanding than impartiality (Gutmann and Thompson 1996), since it only requires that reasons given should be acceptable to others, and not that they must be given from an impersonal, universalistic viewpoint. Individuals do not need to agree with an argument in order to find it acceptable. Acceptability simply means that those reasons cannot be shown to violate the fair terms of cooperation (Gutmann and Thompson 1996: 78) that all citizens should be committed to.

Furthermore, adhering to the principle of reciprocity should still allow individuals to support policies or to object to them based on the effect that they will have on individuals or communities who hold a certain comprehensive doctrine, as these effects would constitute plausible empirical evidence. For example, in a case where certain outcomes or decisions would deeply offend the religious beliefs of some individuals, these individuals could introduce this into the public debate not on the grounds that it offended their God, something which would clearly be a contentious statement, but that it offended them as individuals and failed to offer them the necessary respect that an other-regarding, deliberative decision-making system should offer its citizens. The latter reason would be acceptable in the public forum, as the individuals affected could offer it as evidence of the effects of the decisions. This would be one piece of evidence among many, which could then be weighed in an impartial and other-regarding manner, thus those whose sentiments are easily offended would not be able to veto decisions simply on the grounds that they are offensive to them. Once again, this highlights the key role of other-regarding preferences.

Reciprocity contributes to the legitimacy of deliberative decisions for a number of reasons. First, reciprocity gives the process of deliberation a normative, moral value. Second, citizens are more likely to accept defeat in democratic politics if they feel that their views have received a fair hearing and if they find the reasons offered for this decision acceptable. Third, offering reciprocally acceptable reasons in political discussions is a source of respect. Finally, reciprocity contributes to the development of other-regarding preferences and hence contributes to preference transformation and formation.

Other-Regarding Preferences

Other-regarding preferences are central to the theory of deliberative democracy and are of key importance to its functions of preference formation and preference transformation. These are the ethical or social preferences of individuals which are activated when collective choices need to be made (Goodin and Roberts 1975). Accordingly, ideal deliberation only draws on non-selfish preferences that take account of the effects of decisions on the well-being of others.

Let us consider in more detail what it means to be other-regarding. Other-regarding preferences presuppose a capacity for *empathy*. This empathy needs to be accompanied by a *concern for the welfare of others*: not only do we need to be able to understand the feelings of others, we also need a motivation to react to those feelings. (One could presumably imagine someone who is endowed with empathy, understands others' feelings, but then chooses to use this information to hurt those around him.) These two together enable us to *act* in a non-selfish or other-regarding way. The preference orderings of other-regarding individuals take the preferences and beliefs of others as well as the effects that policies have on others into account (Fung 2004).

Humans appear to be unique in their capability for altruistic behaviour which extends beyond those related to us by blood – even to strangers or members of another species (Silk *et al.* 2005). Actions are altruistic in the strict sense if we help others when this does not benefit us personally and may even prove to be costly. Altruistic behaviour can provide significant psychological benefits to individuals. Experiments using game-theory designs have also shown that significant other-regarding behaviour exists among people (Hoffman *et al.* 1996; Frohlich *et al.* 2004).

It is important to note that other-regardingness does not mean that all arguments presented during debate have to refer to some greater good. Such a requirement would indeed be much too idealistic and it would also disable us from feeling empathy towards others as we would not find out how those others felt. Deliberators should be perfectly free to explain what they believe to be in their best interest, and how a decision would affect them personally. But these claims should be presented as part of an exchange of information that contributes to the function of learning through deliberation, rather than as demands or bargaining chips.

While other-regarding preferences might be present before the start of deliberation, this is not a necessary precondition for its success, as the deliberative procedure itself could trigger their formation. This is what Elster (1998) calls the 'civilizing force of hypocrisy' and Goodin (1986) calls the 'laundering of preferences'. What is necessary is that every group member should respect, or should be forced to respect, the rule that arguments put forward have to be based on more than narrow individual self-interest, or even the interest of a small group. But as deliberation is a repeated process, and individuals have to repeat these other-regarding arguments time and time again, eventually they will genuinely adopt them in order to avoid the cognitive dissonance that thinking one way and arguing another would create (Miller 1992). Thus non-selfish attitudes are created which once again allow groups to work towards the mutually most acceptable outcome. And even if they come to be expressed publicly, selfish or repulsive preferences will be challenged and defeated during the deliberative process (Dryzek 2000). Alternatively, Goodin (1986) suggests that we already hold both egoistic and ethical preferences, and that ethical preferences are already activated in situations where it is rational to do so, like elections or indeed deliberation.

Once again, it is important to emphasize that deliberative democrats only expect an increase in other-regarding attitudes as a result of participating in deliberative discussion, rather than a total and immediate transformation of citizens' preferences (Gutmann and Thompson 1996).

Two Procedural Arguments

Thus the theory of deliberative democracy is characterized by expectations of marked changes in beliefs and preferences. Both procedural and outcome-based justifications of democracy can use this aspect of reasoned deliberation to furnish deliberative decision-making processes with legitimacy. Proceduralists take two main approaches. The first approach is best exemplified by the theories of Habermas (1996a, b) and Dryzek (1990, 2000, 2006), who argue that deliberative or discursive democracy best embodies the values of communicative rationality. The best-known version of the second approach is found in the work of Gutmann and Thompson (1996, 2004), who argue that the legitimacy of deliberative democracy is based on a few of its most salient characteristics, first and foremost reciprocity. Under both of these approaches decision making through reasoned debate is crucial for establishing the legitimacy of democratic processes.

Communicative versus instrumental rationality

The theory of deliberative democracy is often taken to be founded on Habermas's discourse ethics and theory of communicative action. (Here we are concerned with the theory of communicative rationality as it is used in the deliberative democracy literature, where communicative action and rationality take on a broader and less precise meaning, rather than in Habermas's work itself.) For many authors discourse ethics provides the best framework for the validity and legitimacy of deliberative democracy (Benhabib 1996; Dryzek 1990, 2000).

Like most deliberative democrats, Dryzek (2000) sees democracy as an open-ended project and models of democracy as blueprints for further democratization. He argues that this democratization takes place in three directions: increasing the scope of issues subject to deliberative decision-making processes, expanding the range of participants and increasing the *authenticity* of deliberative decision-making processes (Dryzek 1996).

Authenticity is 'the degree to which democratic control is substantive rather than symbolic, informed rather than ignorant and competently engaged' (Dryzek 1996: 5), and '[a]uthentic democracy can be said to exist to the degree that reflective preferences influence collective outcomes' (1996: 2). He argues that currently the most substantial scope for democratization exists in increasing the authenticity of democratic regimes. For Dryzek, this can only be achieved through a deliberative, or as he puts it, discursive model of democracy. Discursive democracy increases legitimacy, facilitating further democratization by widening the control citizens have over politics through the participation of autonomous and competent actors (Dryzek 1996, 2000).

Dryzek then sets out to develop a theory of discursive democracy that takes account of the deliberative turn, but is founded on critical theory rather than liberalism. He sees liberalism as too closely inter-twined with a capitalist mode of production and existing power structures to be able to function as the foundation of a more authentic model of democracy. And if critical theory is the most viable alternative to liberalism, then the most viable alternative to the theory of instrumental rationality dominant in political science is the theory of communicative rationality (Dryzek 1990).

Communicative rationality and instrumental rationality (also referred to as strategic rationality) are often portrayed as competing models, with the former offering a better support for the theory of deliberation than the latter. Instrumental or strategic rationality is the conception of rationality used in economics and it is also widely adopted by political scientists. This is the theory of rationality that forms the basis of rational choice theory and social choice theory as conventionally interpreted. Instrumental rationality takes the ends which individuals want to pursue, that is their preferences, as given. Rational individuals then act based on their beliefs about how to bring those ends about.

According to the thin definition of instrumental rationality used in economics, individual preferences need to satisfy three basic conditions (Varian 1999), which make them representable by *weak orderings*. Specifically, preferences need to be *reflexive,* meaning that each alternative x is weakly preferred to itself (that is, an agent is indifferent between x and itself). Second, preferences need to be *complete*, that is, individuals have to be capable of comparing any two alternatives; formally, for any two alternatives x and y, either x is weakly preferred to y or y is weakly preferred to x (or both). Finally, preferences need to be *transitive*: if an individual weakly prefers x over y and y over z, she will also weakly prefer x over z.

Instrumental rationality is often taken to imply selfish actions in politics that are aimed at maximizing one's own utility without taking into account the interests of others. However, a more precise definition of instrumental rationality that could be derived from the rational choice literature is both narrower and broader than this.

The simplest definition one could give is that instrumentally rational actors choose their actions in a way that will let them achieve their preferred outcome given the beliefs they hold about the consequences of those actions. To give an example, if a student prefers to get a good grade on a course, he will choose studying over going to the cinema to watch a movie unconnected with his studies, as this action is more likely to result in his preferred outcome. Such a definition does not tell us whether the actor's preferences are selfish or not – many people have a preference for seeing others do well – or where those preferences originate. More sophisticated models could take preference formation and change into account as well.

This definition is narrower than the 'selfish actor' definition, because it does not tell us about the normative contents of actors' preferences; their preference could be to help or to harm others or it could be neither. At the same time this makes it also broader, as it can encompass more types of action and allows for non-selfish preferences.

The fact that preferences are usually modelled as constant is more a reflection on the current limitations in modelling techniques than a limitation of the theory of instrumental rationality itself. Preferences are usually held constant in order to simplify the assumptions behind models and to reduce their complexity and newer, more complex models are increasingly accommodating preference change. But there is nothing contradictory between an instrumental conception of rationality and preference change.

Habermas (1984, 1985, 1996a) links instrumental rationality to *strategic action*, which he portrays as a teleological model of action where actors aim to ensure the success of their goals, and in the pursuit of this success adopt an objectifying attitude towards their environment and towards other actors. In contrast, Habermas bases his theory of deliberative democracy on his discourse theory of *communicative action*. Here the focus is on communication and understanding rather than successfully achieving an end. This can then lead to collective problem solving. Furthermore, '[r]eaching an understanding functions as a mechanism for coordinating actions through the participants coming to an agreement concerning the claimed *validity* of their utterances, that is, through intersubjectively recognising the *validity claims* they reciprocally raise' (Habermas 1985: 163, emphasis in original).

When a speaker makes a valid claim he or she claims that his statement is *true*, that the act implied by the statement is *right* with regard to the normative context that the claim is situated in and finally that the intentions of the speaker are *sincere*. Communicative reason makes it possible to make valid claims and to determine when a claim is valid (Habermas 1996a: 5).

The theories of communicative rationality and communicative action offer an explanation of how shared norms develop and are passed on over time, which do not merely appear to serve the narrow interests of the individuals who adhere to them. Accordingly, a commitment to normative standards reached through participating in speech acts can only be adequately explained by communicative rationality (Heath 2001). Agreeing to the reasons behind a normative statement means that we accept that statement. Once this is the case, we are constrained from acting for our own benefit only, as we now have to conform to shared norms. Thus the theory of communicative rationality tells us that we overlook the explanation for social cohesion by referring to instrumental rationality alone. The closest political manifestation of this communicative process is deliberation.

Not all scholars writing on deliberative democracy reject the instrumental conception of rationality. Fung (2003) applies some of the theoretical foundations of rational choice theory in his work, while arguing against a strict rational choice view that does not allow for preference change or the existence of other-regarding preferences.

The Habermasian framework offers us a way in which reason can be considered as a procedural value of democracy. That is, reasoned deliberation is valuable in itself, as an essential component of communicative rationality in politics. But this is not the only framework that can ascribe intrinsic value to reasoned deliberation.

Reasoned deliberation

The second argument for the legitimacy of deliberative democracy based on reasoned debate is also strongly procedural. Here the legitimacy of the deliberative decision-making process is ensured through the normatively desirable properties of reason giving that characterize it. The most sustained version of this theory, which I am going to focus on here, has been put forward by Gutmann and Thompson (1996, 2004). Their work has become extremely influential in the deliberative democracy literature and many of the recent empirical analyses build on their theory of political deliberation.

For Gutmann and Thompson deliberative democracy is a process that is morally legitimate because it arrives at provisionally justified decisions (only provisionally justified, as they could be revised at a later date) that are justifiable to all citizens who are bound by them (1996: 51). They give four reasons why deliberative democracy can achieve this. First, by considering options in a reciprocal, *reasoned* debate, deliberation makes decisions more legitimate under conditions of scarcity:

> The hard choices that democratic governments make under these circumstances should be more acceptable even to those who receive less than they deserve if everyone's claims have been considered on their merits rather than on the basis of wealth, status or power. Even with regard to political decisions with which they disagree, citizens are likely to take a different attitude towards those that are adopted after careful consideration of the relevant conflicting moral claims and those that are adopted only after calculation of the relative strength of the competing political interests. (Gutmann and Thompson 1996: 41–2)

We must note that Gutmann and Thompson are concerned with the morality and legitimacy of democracy in its everyday process, in the ordinary interactions between citizens, civil society, the media, politicians and political institutions. They distance themselves both from pure proceduralists, whom they see as only providing moral foundations for democratic processes, and contractualists, whom they see as concerned with whether democracy arrives at moral outcomes, while both neglect the morality of actual proceedings in everyday democratic politics. Thus for them, even those who get less than they deserve should accept the legitimacy of outcomes if the process through which those outcomes were produced was sufficiently moral. This morality is then derived from fair and reasoned deliberation that is above all reciprocal.

Gutmann and Thompson offer three more arguments in favour of deliberative democracy that are primarily rooted in its reason-giving character. Deliberation encourages citizens to take a broader, more other-regarding view of politics, thereby resulting in a more generous, less selfish and, once again, more moral decision-making process. It also helps citizens to 'distinguish among the moral, the amoral and the immoral' (Gutmann and Thompson 1996: 43) and sort selfish claims from other-regarding ones. Finally, learning through deliberation increases the moral knowledge and understanding of citizens, thereby further reinforcing the justification of decisions. From this brief summary, we can immediately see that the procedural characteristics of deliberative reasoning are of crucial importance for Gutmann and Thompson for making the model of deliberative democracy more legitimate than other models of democracy, and that it achieves this by producing justifiable decisions through a moral process.

Thus, we see that reasoned deliberation is important for procedural justification of democracy, as it is one of the key features that makes deliberative democracy uniquely legitimate for them. Yet if they are important to proceduralists, it makes sense that reasoned deliberation should be doubly important for epistemic theories of democracy.

These theories focus not only on how reasoned debate contributes to the legitimacy and fairness of the decision-making procedure, but also on the way in which it improves the decisions made.

Epistemic Democracy

Epistemic democrats make use of the most prominent outcome-based justification of democracy: that it will arrive at good outcomes, indeed better outcomes than other procedures would produce.

This argument relies on the assumption that some courses of action will always be better than others and in some cases even on the assumption that there is an independently correct or 'true' choice that we ought to try and discover. These theories evaluate decision-making procedures based on how well they track this truth or how likely they are to choose good rather than bad outcomes. The theory that such an independently 'correct' outcome exists is a controversial one (Peter 2007a).

Politics deals with questions to which we usually do not know the right answer. Most of us in modern democracies can agree on shared goals and values; the importance of quality education and healthcare for all, poverty reduction, a preference for peace over war. Where we differ is our belief as to how these aims can be achieved.

In order to avoid making controversial evaluations, one of the prime proponents of the epistemic value of democracy, David Estlund (2008), proposes to use the concept of primary bads. These are things that we can universally agree are bad: war, disease, famine, genocide. Any system of government can then be evaluated for how likely it is to avoid these primary bads. This is similar to the theory that argues for democracy based on the grounds that genuinely democratic countries do not go to war with each other (Ray 1998) and Sen's (1982) famous study that showed that democratic countries were better at avoiding famine. Ultimately, even if we reject moral realism and do not accept that difficult moral and political questions will always have one independently correct answer, it is still possible to argue that some decisions will leave us collectively better off than others.

If we are interested in choosing the best possible decision, then we might consider leaving decision making to the wise or the experts, as in Plato's *Republic*. This idea is called *epistocracy*. A more contemporary version of this is technocratic government that delegates decisions about reaching certain goals to experts and bureaucrats. Epistocracy may be appealing if we believe we can delegate decision making to benevolent and wise rulers. But even then, it may not be acceptable on procedural grounds. Autonomy and self-government are important values for governing both the lives of individuals and societies.

The most compelling argument against epistocracy from a democratic perspective is what David Estlund (2008) calls the expert/boss fallacy. Just because someone is an expert on an issue, this it does not mean that he or she has any authority to make binding decisions for us. This is important, because in a state such decisions are enforced through coercive laws.

If I believe as an individual that my doctor is sufficiently knowledgeable and trustworthy to make important decisions for me about aspects of my lifestyle, such as my diet, then I will carry out his orders as I believe that he is an expert on this issue and will give me good advice. However, as a society we are very unlikely to agree who the experts are on any issue, let alone on all issues. Who is the expert on abortion, for example? Doctors, researchers, the Pope or maybe mothers? Given this disagreement, we will not be able to authorize any expert collectively to make decisions on our behalf legitimately.

In respect of legitimacy, democracy fares much better than epistocracy. While we may not be able to agree which experts to authorize to make our decisions for us, reasonable individuals can agree on the fairness of an equal and collective method of decision making, such as democratic voting. This solves the problem of authorization. However, epistemic democrats would argue that democratic decision making is not only fair, but also good at identifying the truth. As a society, collectively we will not do much worse than the experts. '[Democracy] is not an infallible procedure, and there might even be more accurate procedures. But democracy is better than random and is epistemically the best among those that are generally acceptable in the way that political legitimacy requires.' (Estlund 2008: 8) Thus it should come as no surprise that deliberative democracy can also be justified on epistemic grounds.

The best-known epistemic justification of democratic *voting* is the Condorcet Jury Theorem (Goodin 2003; Condorcet 1994; Grofman *et al.* 1988). At the end of the eighteenth century, Condorcet argued that if a group of people who are better than random at choosing correctly vote independently of each other about the correctness of two options, they are much more likely to arrive at a good outcome than each individual would be on their own. Bayes's theorem states that reasonable individuals will adjust their beliefs about the probability that a proposition is true when they receive new evidence as to its correctness. Votes or arguments made by other citizens can be seen as such pieces of evidence.

However, these theories do not apply straightforwardly to deliberative democracy. In particular, deliberation violates some of the key conditions of the Condorcet Jury Theorem. Not only do deliberators not vote independently of each other, but their votes are influenced by the arguments that others have presented during the deliberative process. Moreover we can expect that their judgements and thereby their individual competences have all changed in the same direction, either towards or away from the correct or best solution. The Jury

Theorem in its current form cannot be applied to deliberation, although other similar theoretical models may yet fulfill this role (Dietrich and Spiekermann, 2010).

One epistemic defence of deliberative democracy comes from pragmatist quarters. Pragmatists such as Misak (2000) and Talisse (2005) argue that the value of deliberative democracy lies in creating an ongoing debate in search of the truth that satisfies the requirements of pragmatic inquiry. But the most important epistemic justification of deliberative democracy is that it gives power to the best argument.

The power of the best argument

According to deliberative democrats it is the 'power of the best argument' (Habermas 1996a) that delivers the greatest epistemic improvement. Ideally deliberators will arrive at their judgements through carefully considering the arguments presented during the debate. And according to deliberative democrats, democratic deliberation allows us to judge the strength of arguments better due to the time and attention we devote to examining them. Deliberation might then be a unique moment in the political process when our viewpoints might be challenged and we might be more willing to engage in deep reflection.

Habermas (2003) argues that in our day-to-day lives we treat our knowledge as certain and act as if our beliefs were true. We need to have such a non-epistemic conception of truth in order to accomplish the tasks that we are faced with. But there are times when such unproblematic, naïve beliefs need to be challenged through dialogue. Discursive truth is established at such times of deliberation. For Habermas this is how non-epistemic or everyday truth is connected to a more coherent and epistemically more rigorous version of truth.

Democratic deliberation is exactly such a discursive process. It is easy to hold incoherent or unjustified views if citizen participation in democratic decision making consists only of voting. This would give people little incentive to seek out the views of others, reducing the extent to which they talked about politics with those with different beliefs and preferences (Mutz 2006). If citizens only talk to people who hold the same views as they do, then they will always go unchallenged and will indeed be confirmed in their beliefs. But if they take part in deliberation, provided that all views are properly represented, they will necessarily be confronted by viewpoints which are different from theirs. They will also be obliged to present and justify their arguments to others, who will be allowed to question and critique what they have said (Gutmann and Thompson 1996, 2004). This can be aided by introducing new information and learning new facts during deliberation (Manin 1987). Discussion also enables individuals to learn more about each other. Without deliberation people know much about their own preferences and interests, but little about those of others (Nino 1996).

This process should lead us to recognize the inconsistencies and weaknesses in our arguments. And not only would it help us to revise our own arguments, but it would also introduce us to new arguments which we and others could investigate freely. This, it is argued, would surely lead to the discovery of a better argument than voting on its own could do. Of course one would assume that arguments would need to be subjected to such a process repeatedly, echoing the position of Barber (1984) or Benhabib (1996).

Epistemic proceduralism

While democracy might be a good method of arriving at good decisions most of the time, it is far from infallible. Given the contentious nature of political problems and the complexity of the decision-making processes, it is not even possible to tell how often democratic processes can give us better decisions than non-democratic ones. Thus we need to find grounds for accepting the legitimacy of those decisions even if we suspect that they are wrong. Procedural justifications of democracy achieve just this. As we have seen above, these justifications have already been used in arguments against epistocracy. The decisions of 'experts' may be correct most of the time but that does not make them legitimate rulers, unless all reasonable people can agree on their expertise.

However, we may not wish to let go of the epistemic justification of democracy entirely. If nothing else, we may wish our theory of democracy to reflect this salient feature of the decision-making process. This is just what epistemic proceduralism aims to achieve (Estlund 2008; Peter 2007a). These accounts acknowledge that epistemic and procedural accounts of democracy are impossible to divorce from each other entirely.

According to Estlund (2008), laws or decisions which we believe to be wrong should be obeyed because they were brought about by a procedure which, while imperfect, is still epistemically valuable. Thus the legitimacy of decisions derives from the procedure through which they were made. For Estlund democracy's epistemic value is derived from the fact that we will make better decisions if we deliberate together. Real-life deliberation can be compared against an ideal model of epistemic deliberation, but it will not and should not mirror it. Estlund argues that democratic decision-making procedures that make use of such deliberation will not only arrive at decisions which are better than random at avoiding the worst disasters or primary bads that can befall humankind, such as war, famine or genocide, but that they are not too much worse at doing so than non-democratic procedures would be. This makes democratic decisions authoritative, meaning that they have the moral power to require obedience. As these epistemically valuable decisions also fulfil the constraints of legitimacy, democratic processes fulfil the dual role of arriving at good decisions through a procedure that is acceptable to all reasonable persons.

Peter (2007a) criticizes Estlund's model of epistemic proceduralism for relying on an independently available, objective standard of correctness. She wants to show that justifications based on epistemic proceduralism can be established without requiring such an independent standard. For this she uses a social epistemological approach that places the emphasis on the knowledge-producing practices that lead to a decision and defines knowledge and knowing in the context of these practices. She argues that Young's (2000) model of deliberative democracy implicitly uses such a model of social epistemology by requiring that all groups in society should be given a voice in the deliberative procedure. These different voices are a resource that leads to knowledge-producing practices that take a fuller account of differing views and knowledge bases in society. Thus these processes can be argued to be epistemically valuable without drawing on an independent standard of correctness.

Epistemic proceduralism offers a viable alternative to both purely procedural and purely epistemic justifications of democracy. However, it still relies primarily on epistemic justification, falling back on proceduralism in order to account for borderline cases and cases where there is reasonable disagreement over the goodness of an outcome. Thus it is still open to criticisms of the epistemic strength of deliberation.

Problems of epistemic democracy

But does the best argument always triumph in democratic deliberation? Many of the criticisms levelled against the deliberative theory of democracy focus on the logical and cognitive weaknesses of its participants and the likelihood that these weaknesses may not lead to better decisions than would other forms of democratic decision making, such as voting.

The social sciences have catalogued a large number of cognitive biases and logical fallacies that humans are prone to. Most of these are more relevant for deliberation than for other methods of democratic decision making. A powerful example is the confirmation bias: we are more likely to accept arguments which already support our existing position than arguments which contradict it, regardless of the strengths of those arguments. Recent research suggests that some of these biases might even have neurological bases, for example our tendency towards optimism when it comes to our assessment of the likelihood that bad things such as serious illness will happen to us (Sharot *et al*. 2011).

Pincione and Tesón (2006) argue that democratic deliberation is affected by 'discourse failure', or a failure to judge arguments based on their real merits. According to them, this often takes the form of a bias towards vivid arguments that consist of imagery that is easy to understand and assigns causality to specific actors, when the true state of the world is best described by opaque arguments, which are difficult to understand and make use of invisible-hand mechanisms. As an example, when petrol prices go up, vivid arguments blame greedy oil companies, whereas opaque arguments refer to forces of supply and demand.

Individual citizens are likely to accept vivid arguments even when they are honest and well-intentioned, as they are not rationally motivated to learn enough to understand opaque ones. Politicians use vivid arguments as they are more accessible to citizens and have a greater emotional appeal, as well as allowing them to appear as agents of change in situations when they are in reality powerless in the face of impersonal forces. Finally, discourse failure is fuelled by the fact that politics is about redistributing resources, whether power or money, and interest groups will refer to vivid arguments to claim their rights to them. However, one cannot fail to notice that the thrust of this argument is that non-specialists will often favour simple arguments over the complicated ones presented by specialists and academics when the latter are correct; yet this relation cannot always hold.

One bias that could be particularly likely to affect deliberation is conformity. Conformity is a rational reaction in many different situations (Sunstein 2003). Individuals sometimes follow others when they do not have enough information to make up their mind, when they want to protect their reputation, or when they do not want to upset those they care about. Despite being aware of the dangers of conformity (Elster 1986), most deliberative democrats still dismiss the possibility that it will cause problems for deliberation, without justifying this assertion properly.

Furthermore, privileging the power of the best argument may have adverse effects for minorities (Young 2000). It may lead to a style of deliberation that is more reminiscent of discussions in the seminar room and privileges those who have been trained to articulate well-reasoned and logically rigorous arguments. At the same time, those who do not conform to the expected style of debate may not be taken seriously, no matter how right or valid their arguments are. Thus focusing on the power of the best argument may lead to a decrease in equality and inclusion.

I will now examine two of the biases to highlight the problems they cause for the theory of deliberative democracy: framing and group polarization.

Framing

Individuals often reach different judgements when the same choice is presented to them in two different formats. This phenomenon is known as framing and has been studied extensively by social psychologists and economists. Citizens will respond differently to questions about political issues according to how they are framed. While they say in opinion polls that the US should seek permission from the United Nations Security Council before going to war, they do not agree that the US needs the permission of Russia or China, which are both powerful permanent members of the Council (Fang 2008).

In a well-known experiment by Kahnemann and Tversky (1979, 1984) subjects preferred different courses of action as a response to the outbreak of an infectious disease, depending on the way in which the scenario was described to them. They preferred certainty when it came to saving lives, but accepted a gamble about the number of deaths.

In the first scenario, adopting the first programme meant that 200 people would definitely be saved, and adopting the second programme meant that there was a one-third probability that all 600 people would be saved and two-thirds probability that no one would be saved. In the second scenario, adopting the first programme meant that 400 people would die for certain, and adopting the second programme meant that there was a one-third probability that no one would die and two-thirds probability that everyone would die. It is easy to see that the two scenarios are identical, except for the way in which the two programmes are described. However subjects tended to prefer the first programme in the first scenario and the second programme in the second scenario.

Kahnemann and Tversky (1979) explain this using prospect theory; we have value functions that are concave in the domain of gains and convex in the domain of losses. Thus we are risk-averse when it comes to gains (lives saved) and risk-seeking when we consider losses (lives lost). This behaviour is not strictly instrumentally rational as it violates von Neumann and Morgenstern's (1947) principle of *substitution*, which would require that if x is preferred to y then an even chance of getting x or z is preferred to an even chance of getting y or z. It also violates the principle of *invariancy,* as information is processed differently and different decisions are reached depending on the way in which a problem is presented. These findings have been further generalized to include the attributes of single options and goals. We prefer minced meat that is labelled '75 per cent meat' to that which is labelled '25 per cent fat' (Lewin and Gaeth 1988), and women are more likely to practise breast self-examination if they are told that the rate of early detection of breast cancer is lower without it, rather than when they are told that it is higher with it (Meyerowitz and Chaiken 1987).

Framing is at work too when a problem can be presented using two conflicting sets of concepts or values; for example, regulating pesticides can be seen as an environmental triumph or an economic burden.

If, as assumed by its proponents, deliberative democracy is indeed subject to reciprocity and enhances other-regarding attitudes, this can lead to the emergence of a common framing or paradigm which would displace private arguments (Bohman 1996). Accordingly, a new discourse that all sub-groups could use and access would create a bridge between different moral discourses that have trouble understanding each other.

The dominance of one way of framing an issue has a serious impact on the decisions of a deliberative group. Such a common framing could negate assumptions about the openness of deliberation and the use of discussion to present multiple sides of a debate, as there could be strong pressure within the group to adopt the common framing. Framing could also be used to present issues in a way that serves our own preferred outcomes best and a way in which we can manipulate the discussion by emphasizing one aspect of the issue over others. This clearly does not conform to the expectations of deliberative democrats.

Of course, one can argue that framing is just a natural way of constructing a shared understanding that enables us to communicate with each other and with which we can make sense of the world. Such a construct would reduce complexity, making it easier for us to understand issues which may otherwise lie beyond our cognitive capacities, and allow us to make deliberation with each other meaningful. On its own, framing is value neutral; it is neither a good thing nor a bad thing.

Group polarization

Democratic deliberation can also be biased through two forms of 'groupthink': group polarization and informational cascades, the effects of which have been extensively studied by Cass Sunstein (2002, 2003).

Group polarization occurs when individual preferences become more intense or extreme due to discussion with like-minded people. If a group of people favouring gun control meets to discuss this issue, they are likely to become more avid supporters of gun control laws after the discussion than they had been beforehand.

There are two main reasons for this. First, hearing arguments from those who already agree with us means we are less likely to be introduced to opposing arguments. Thus, the pool of available arguments is biased towards individuals' existing opinions. Second, people will be confirmed in the acceptability and validity of their initial views. Meeting with peers and discovering that they hold the same views as us allows people to feel more secure in the social acceptability of their initial convictions and to carry those convictions even further.

Evidence for group polarization can be found in jury studies (Sunstein 2002). This can be most clearly seen in cases where mock juries were asked to award damages to plaintiffs from companies.

After jury deliberation, the level of damages favoured by jury members was statistically significantly higher than those favoured without discussion.

While it biases group deliberation, in itself group polarization does not indicate that the quality of the decision made will be lowered. If a group of schoolchildren discuss the implications of a globe-shaped Earth revolving around the sun, their increased conviction of these basic scientific facts will most likely benefit them. However, a meeting of the Flat Earth Society does not benefit its members by making them believe more fervently that the Earth is flat.

Deliberation will sometimes work in this way, as people realize through discussion that their original, reasonable beliefs and intuitions are shared by others and therefore their confidence in their belief increases. If these initial beliefs are correct, this is an unproblematic process. However, in politics we often face issues where there is reasonable disagreement among people. In these cases, in order to avoid bias, deliberation should ideally take place among people from a variety of backgrounds and with a variety of views.

In micro deliberation, this can be ensured through sampling and careful selection of participants. However, we face a problem if participants are self-selected and the meeting attracts those who already hold strong and similar views on an issue or if only people from one side of the debate are motivated to attend.

We face even more serious challenges in the case of macro deliberation. Most people like to avoid confrontation (Hibbing and Theiss-Morse 2002) and will most likely associate with people who hold similar views to them. Thus, macro deliberation can often be a case of bonding, rather than bridging views. This tendency can be clearly seen in the political Internet community. Both current affairs blogs and political discussion forums tend to attract readers who already agree with the tone of the website and link to other sites with similar views to theirs. This creates *echo chambers* where people's initial views on issues are repeatedly confirmed and never or rarely challenged (Sunstein 2007).

Informational cascades occur when we make decisions based on the actions or beliefs of others, even when those actions or beliefs are not well-informed or carefully considered. Most of us will have faced a situation where we had to pick a restaurant in a town or area that was not familiar to us. In these cases people often use simple heuristics, such as the number of people already sitting in a restaurant.

However, those others may also be unfamiliar with the area and could have chosen the restaurant randomly themselves, maybe based on its name or the colour of the tablecloths.

This decision-making bias is exacerbated by a cascade effect. As more people jump on the bandwagon, the action or belief becomes more convincing to others and as a result even more people adopt the original, ill-considered position. As we have seen above, in circumstances where each individual choice is likely to be correct, we can assume that a large number of people choosing individually will make a good decision. This is supported by both Condorcet's and Bayes's theorems. However, in the case of informational cascades a number of conditions of these theorems are missing. First, individuals are not necessarily more likely to be right than wrong. Second, people do not make up their minds independently. Instead, they follow the choices of others, thereby reducing the actual group size to that of the original choosers. Hardly a triumph for the better argument.

Conclusion

The extent to which these biases damage the epistemic credentials of deliberation is debatable. It is certain that real-life deliberation will be prone to many of them and that they will at times affect the final outcome of the decision-making process. How frequently and to what extent they will be present is not yet known and requires further study. Of course this does not mean that deliberation will not have epistemic benefits. But we do not yet have much beyond intuition and common sense to confirm this. This gives procedural accounts of the value of deliberative democracy advantages that the epistemic accounts do not have.

First, since it is the focus on the procedure of deliberation that gives the theory of deliberative democracy its unique appeal, it is much easier to argue for the model based on the intrinsic values of that deliberation itself. This is indeed what most deliberative democrats have done so far.

Second, it is difficult to observe whether decisions made through deliberation are better or more correct than decisions made through other methods would have been. The questions asked in political deliberation will not be easy ones and there will not be straightforward answers to them. It is much easier to observe whether deliberation fulfills its procedural values and base the legitimacy of the procedure on those. If we want to preserve an epistemic justification of democracy, this will then point towards epistemic proceduralism as the best route to doing so.

The next chapter will examine a procedural justification of deliberative democracy: the fact that it ought to consist of *uncoerced, equal and inclusive* debate.

4
Equality and Inclusion

Equality and inclusion are valuable for theories of democracy because they are necessary to ensure legitimacy. We have a stronger reason for accepting laws and policies, especially laws and policies that we disagree with, if we know that our interests have been treated equally with those of others (Christiano 1996, 2004) and if we believe that we were included in the decision-making process. Furthermore, being treated as equals and being given equal respect as human beings and moral agents is a fundamental tenet of liberalism.

As I have shown in earlier chapters, the theory of deliberative democracy lies at the intersection of multiple research traditions. This is especially evident in the case of equality and inclusion. Deliberative democrats have different conceptions of these values and while these conceptions are not contradictory, they create tensions within the theory.

First, democratic theorists have been concerned for decades with the question of how democratic decision making can be made equal and who the members of a polity should be. Second, some deliberative democrats are concerned with the kind of equality that is necessary to make deliberation just or fair. These theorists engage with the debate about what it means to be equal in a just society. Third, some theorists follow Habermas and interpret deliberative democracy as the political application of speech act theory. These theorists focus on the power of the best argument and put less emphasis on equality and inclusion. Finally, difference democrats have identified a number of issues that force us to re-think how we integrate these values into a model of democracy.

While inclusion and equality are seen as key values by all deliberative democrats, they are particularly important for *difference democrats*. Difference democrats are theorists who are concerned with the political implications of structural inequalities and power differences in society. Such inequalities exist between men and women, between different cultural groups in a pluralist society or between different social classes. They create what Williams (1998) terms 'marginalised ascriptive groups'. Individuals become members of these groups by birth rather than by choice and they are often judged negatively or suffer discrimination based on their membership.

After defining non-coercion, equality and inclusion in the next section, I will examine inclusion and equality in greater detail and assess how these values can be guaranteed by a deliberative form of democracy.

Uncoerced, Inclusive and Equal Discussion

Lack of coercion (Cohen 1989) is the easiest to define of the three procedural values discussed in this chapter. A deliberative discussion is uncoerced if none of the deliberators face either implicit or explicit threats from others aimed at changing their behaviour. Freedom from coercion also means that no one may be ostracized from deliberative politics because of their views. Coercion may lead to the suppression of arguments and viewpoints, and threats may lead deliberators to change their judgements in order to save face or to conform.

Non-coercion plays an important normative role in deliberative theory. Only if deliberators are able to present their own arguments, judgements, political opinions and preferences in deliberation will the outcome of such a process be truly deliberative. This is because deliberation relies on reason giving, information pooling and learning about each other's arguments and beliefs to achieve a transformation of preferences. If deliberators are not free to present and justify their judgements in public, this process will be hampered. Thus, if minorities are not able to speak freely and without coercion in a deliberative forum, their point of view cannot be shared with the rest of society.

Parallel to the threat of coercion is the threat of *bribery*. Deliberators may be unduly influenced not only by sticks, but also by carrots. Deliberators should not be tempted into adopting the arguments of others for material benefits unrelated to the policies that the deliberative forum decides on. This is analogous to the idea that citizens' votes should not be bought. Coercion and bribery are morally illegitimate, as they change the incentive structures of citizens so that they are tempted to trade off short-term gains against their real interests and the interests of the community.

Lack of coercion is such a fundamental ideal of democratic politics that it is often taken for granted. However, it is important to make sure that institutional arrangements minimize coercion and bribery as much as possible. Secret ballots were introduced for exactly this reason. In deliberative democracy, such secrecy is not always possible as the nature of discussion in politics ensures that individuals publicly offer judgements that will be known to all participants (see Chapter 5). Publicity plays a crucial role in deliberative democracy, as it is the basis on which deliberators are required to justify their judgements and on which arguments for final decisions have to be made available to all. However, publicity is only meaningful if it is set against a background of non-coercion.

Non-coercion is a background condition that is necessary to ensure equality and inclusion, the two main procedural values examined in this chapter. These two conditions raise new and interesting questions for deliberative democracy that purely electoral forms of democracy did not have to face. The first of these is *who* and *what* should be equal and included.

When it comes to inclusion and equality, most models of democracy focus on people, rather than ideas. Equality centres on assuring citizens' equal moral worth through allowing everyone to participate in the political process in order to advance their interests. Concerns about exclusion are concerns about denying members of minorities their rights, rather than ignoring ideas and arguments. However, this is not sufficient for deliberative models of democracy.

Deliberative theories of democracy are not only concerned with people, but also with arguments and ideas. This is especially evident in the Habermasian strand of the theory (Habermas 1996a). Deliberative democracy is conceptualized as collective political rule through discussion and theorists frequently invoke the power the best argument is supposed to have in such a discussion. Thus when it comes to the values of equality and inclusion, we need to consider not only what it means for citizens to be equal and included during deliberation, but also what this means for ideas, facts and arguments.

This interpretation of democratic equality and inclusion, however, does not sit together easily with ideas about the politics of presence (Phillips 1995) or descriptive representation (Mansbridge 1999a). These theories emphasize the physical inclusion of those groups which have been traditionally excluded from politics, such as women or minorities. They argue that it is not enough to have these groups' interests represented if they themselves cannot be included in the political process. The theory of deliberative democracy has to balance the sometimes contradictory requirements of the politics of presence and the politics of the best argument.

Keeping this in mind, we can now attempt to define inclusion and equality in the deliberative context. I will start with inclusion, since just as a lack of coercion is necessary to make inclusion and equality meaningful, so equality makes little sense if the conditions of inclusion do not exist that allow members of society to make use of it.

The procedural value of *inclusion* ensures that all those citizens who are substantively affected by a decision or policy have the right and the opportunity to participate, and all relevant arguments have an opportunity to be presented in the deliberative process. It is important to note, however, that although we may be affected by an issue even by just reading about it in a newspaper, we may not necessarily be affected by it in a more substantive sense. One of the aims of the theory of deliberative democracy is to give minorities who are currently excluded from political decision-making processes a voice (Benhabib 1996; Young 2000; Fung and Wright 2003). In order to do this, deliberative democracy would need to include both *persons* from minority groups and *viewpoints and arguments* from minorities.

Two aspects of inclusion are crucial for deliberative democracy. The first is inclusion when the deliberative group is constituted. The second is inclusion during the deliberative process itself. Iris Marion Young (2000) calls these two *external* and *internal* inclusion respectively. External inclusion is ensured if we make sure that all affected individuals are invited to deliberative meetings and that they have the means to attend. Internal inclusion refers to making sure that all participants of the deliberative debate are actually allowed to and able to voice their views during the debate.

Deliberation also needs to be characterized by *equality*. The most common conception of equality in democratic thought is the idea of 'one person, one vote'. Even in liberal representative democracies this leaves plenty of scope for inequality, as it only allows for equality between citizens in the act of voting for their political representatives. Needless to say, this conception of equality is completely inapplicable to deliberative democracy.

There is no consensus on how equality in deliberation should be defined (Bohman 1997; Knight and Johnson 1997; Peter 2007b). Unlike minimal models of democracy, the theory of deliberative democracy has to face the *equality of what* question. Answers to this question include equality of influence, opportunities, capabilities or primary goods. These conceptions of equality originate from contemporary debates on egalitarianism and justice.

It helps to define equality in deliberative democracy if we differentiate between two types. *Formal equality* defines the minimal political rights that all citizens must possess in equal measure in order to be real participants in the political process. *Substantive equality* means that citizens have roughly equal power, abilities and opportunities to influence political decisions. In liberal representative democracies, giving each citizen one vote ensures equality in the formal, minimal sense. At the same time, large substantive inequalities may continue to exist among the electorate. Most prominently, some may be able to provide candidates and parties with substantial financial support, while the vast majority of the population will not be able to do so.

The requirements of inclusion and equality together make deliberation democratic. Equality ensures that each citizen has the right, either formal or substantive, to speak and be heard by others. Inclusion ensures that citizens have the opportunity to make use of these rights in practice. 'When coupled with norms of political equality, inclusion allows for maximum expression of interests, opinions, and perspectives relevant to the problems or issues for which a public seeks a solution.' (Young 2000: 23)

In the rest of the chapter I will explore all types of inclusion and equality as they relate to both people and ideas. As we shall see, not all forms of equality and inclusion are possible or desirable in all circumstances. I will start by discussing inclusion, before moving on to equality.

Inclusion

The external inclusion of citizens

Social exclusion and political exclusion are related concepts. Individuals are socially excluded if they do not have the opportunity to participate in the normal activities of citizens of a country. This usually includes enjoying reasonable living standards and a sense of security, participating in paid employment or other valued activities, being able to make decisions and drawing support from friends, family and the wider community (Burchardt *et al.* 2002). Political participation is one of the activities that normal citizens of democratic countries engage in, therefore being excluded from politics is a form of social exclusion.

Political exclusion can be the result of discrimination based on a variety of characteristics, such as gender, class or race. It can be the consequence either of the design of a political system or of poor opportunities for some groups in society to participate in politics (Phillips 1995: 1). Examples of the first type of political exclusion include tying voting rights to literacy, requirements for advance voter registration, electoral systems designed in a way that makes the election of minority representatives difficult (Phillips 1995) or the difficulty with which immigrants obtain citizenship in some countries (Sen 2000).

But even without such obstacles, the second type of political exclusion, a restriction of opportunities to participate, may be present. Political deals are often struck in back rooms, benefiting those who are already most powerful in society (Young 2000). Those in the lower socio-economic strata in society are less likely to vote as they do not see the significance of doing so (Electoral Commission and Hansard Society 2007), and when it comes to more active political participation than just voting, political exclusion can be even more widespread. In the United States those not receiving benefit payments are more than twice as likely to participate in politics as citizens receiving food stamps (Verba *et al.* 1995: 209). Lacking free time, motivation or material preconditions can reduce a person's likelihood of being able to get involved in politics: 'Such preconditions are not met, for example, in the case of the unemployed single mother on an out-of-town housing estate who cannot afford costs of political equality such as babysitting, transport and meals out' (Barry 2002: 22).

What makes political exclusion so problematic (Young 2000) is that together with individuals, entire social perspectives – such as those of minorities or women – are excluded from the political arena. Social perspective is the shared framework that individuals from a similar position in society use to interpret events. It develops as a result of experience, history and social knowledge. While a social perspective offers a common interpretative framework, not all who share it will arrive at the same conclusions. As an example, Young argues that the *Pittsburgh Courier* has a recognizable African American voice, even though its contributors range from liberals to conservatives. Excluding some social perspectives from democratic deliberation leads to an impoverishment of political life and a serious disadvantage in public representation for those whose viewpoints are not present. Making sure that all such social perspectives are adequately included in political decision making can certainly be seen as one of the key aims of the deliberative democracy project.

In order to be inclusive, deliberative democracy needs to fulfill two key requirements, which correspond to the two types of political exclusion defined above. First, the process of selecting deliberators must be inclusive, and second, all deliberators must have the practical ability to attend deliberative meetings.

In order to think about inclusion it is important to identify who is entitled to participate in the deliberative process. This question is easier to answer for a macro model of democratic deliberation, where deliberation would permeate society and would encompass citizens, the media, civil society organizations, politicians and all branches of government. Here, the question is less about selecting participants than about identifying who should be present as a first step in removing obstacles to participation for different groups.

The key participants of macro deliberation are citizens, politicians, the government, civil society and the media. All members of society have to have the opportunity to become members of each of these categories. This is violated if members of some groups have little or no chance of becoming politicians, setting up civil society groups or working in government organizations or for the media. Inclusive macro deliberation also requires that all citizens of a political community should have opportunities to communicate with each of these other participants in the deliberative debate. This need not imply universal participation. As long as key stakeholders have an opportunity to participate, macro deliberation will satisfy the condition of external inclusion.

In macro deliberative procedures external inclusion primarily consists of providing opportunities for citizens to participate, rather than actively selecting deliberators. In micro deliberation, on the other hand, selecting those who will participate in the deliberative proceedings is the key stage at which external inclusion is ensured. Micro deliberation consists of face-to-face meetings about a well-defined topic, between well-defined participants. If we assume that micro deliberation takes place in elected legislatures, inclusive participant selection becomes a question of inclusive electoral representation. A more important problem is posed if deliberation takes place among ordinary citizens.

Many local deliberative meetings, such as town hall meetings or planning permission meetings, are self-selecting. As long as they are adequately publicized in advance, their inclusiveness can be ensured by making sure that all those who have an interest in attending have the opportunity to do so.

For the deliberative meetings inspired by the theoretical literature, selecting which citizens should participate in deliberation is often seen as a question of sampling. Currently more serious deliberative endeavours, such as deliberative polls or the British Columbia Citizens' Assembly, use random sampling to ensure that a representative cross-section of society is present during deliberation (Fishkin *et al.* 2007; Gastil 2000). These sampling methods are designed explicitly to make sure that all segments of the population are offered a chance to participate; therefore they satisfy the requirement for external inclusion. Of course, it is possible that there could be a systematic bias in non-respondents in these deliberative polls, that is, attendees and non-attendees are in some statistically significant way different from each other. As I will argue shortly, this is unavoidable and need not necessarily pose a serious problem for these projects. An ambitious extension of such cross-sectional representation would be the actual involvement of the entire population of voting age, as in Ackermann and Fishkin's (2004) deliberation day or Leib's (2004) deliberative jury duty.

But it is not enough to invite all relevant individuals to the deliberative debate. This would remain a meaningless gesture if we did not actually ensure that people would be able to attend the meeting. This poses a more serious difficulty. There are further barriers to participation that can lead to political exclusion. First, some citizens will lack or be unwilling to sacrifice time, money and other resources to attend meetings. Second, individuals may not have the motivation to attend or they may feel that they lack the necessary level of political efficacy for participation. Not all of these problems can be remedied easily through institutional measures (see Chapter 6 for further discussion of institutional responses to these questions).The two problems of time and financial resources are often interlinked, as in the case of those who have to work long hours or multiple jobs to make a living.

This is not necessarily limited to those from poorer backgrounds, but occurs across the socio-economic spectrum; many professionals also work long hours that may preclude them from attending deliberative meetings or participating in political activities. Those suffering from financial hardship may not be able to afford the cost of childcare or transport. This can affect participation in both micro and macro deliberation. In 2007, 32 per cent of British citizens said that they were too busy and lacked the time to participate actively in politics (Electoral Commission and Hansard Society 2007). Results from participatory projects in Brazil show that working women were less likely to participate as they had to juggle both work and household responsibilities (Baiocchi 2003).

It is possible to lower this first barrier through institutional arrangements. Deliberative meetings would need to be held at a time and place that was accessible to all. Some schemes envisage offering cash incentives to citizens to encourage and enable them to take part in deliberation. This echoes the ancient Athenian practice of paying citizens to participate in politics. Ackermann and Fishkin (2004) propose offering each citizen $150 for attending deliberation day. Gastil (2000) would also offer cash incentives for participants to cover costs such as travel or childcare. Both of these schemes also provide deliberators with free time to attend either in the form of a national holiday (Ackermann and Fishkin 2004) or leave from work that is analogous to that taken for jury duties (Gastil 2000). But these institutional means can only go so far and lack of time and money could continue to lead to political exclusion.

Not only is offering cash incentives or national holidays very costly, but it is questionable how many people would sacrifice a new bank holiday in order to attend a political meeting. Studies have shown that people are more risk-averse when it comes to losses rather than gains (Kahnemann and Tversky 1979), that is, they are more reluctant to lose a holiday than they are enthusiastic about gaining one. Citizens could quickly come to see participating in deliberation as a costly activity that would lead them to lose a holiday, even if they would not have had this holiday in the first place without the existence of the deliberative institution.

The second problem leading to political exclusion is that the most disadvantaged members of society often lack political efficacy, interest in politics and motivation to participate in politics. Political efficacy captures the extent to which citizens believe that they are able to influence politics and that the political system represents their best interests. Those with low political efficacy will believe that participating in politics is futile, as their actions will have little effect on outcomes. They may also feel that they lack the abilities and skills needed for success. Or they may simply be unfamiliar with their rights and feel that politics is irrelevant to them. As citizens withdraw from political life, their views are not adequately represented, thereby marginalizing them even further and making their participation in politics even less likely. Only 37 per cent of people in the two lowest socio-economic groups in the UK say that they are interested in politics, whereas in the two highest socio-economic groups 76 per cent claim to have such interests (Electoral Commission and Hansard Society 2006) (for analogous results in the US, see Verba *et al.* 1995: 348–50).

Deliberative democrats could respond to this form of political exclusion by explicitly involving disadvantaged groups in deliberative decision making and thereby showing them that they can make a difference. Indeed, this has been the aim of a number of recent deliberative projects, such as school boards and neighbourhood policing schemes (Fung 2004), the participatory budget procedures in Porto Alegre (Baiocchi 2003) or the campaign for democratic decentralization in Kerala (Isaac and Heller 2003). Archon Fung calls this form of deliberation 'empowered participatory governance' or 'empowered deliberative democracy' (Fung 2004, Fung and Wright 2003). The aim of empowered deliberative democracy is to involve ordinary people in a deliberative procedure aimed at solving everyday, tangible problems that affect their lives. Thus decision making over specific local issues is moved from distant bureaucracies or political parties to local residents. Not only does this empower these residents to make positive changes to their lives, but it also facilitates the development of better cooperation between groups and individuals (Fung and Wright 2003: 18).

How far deliberative democrats would be successful in achieving these aims is still debatable, but it is undoubtedly one of the most attractive features of the theory of deliberative democracy that it explicitly aims to include the most politically disadvantaged and disaffected groups. Their inclusion would both increase the legitimacy of democratic political processes and help the worst off in society by representing their interests more accurately and effectively.

It is impossible to ensure that everyone will participate in deliberative democratic processes. Even when we give all relevant members of a political community the opportunity to participate, some will choose not to do so. This is true for all forms of deliberation, whether macro or micro and whether the participants are selected by organizers or self-selected. Thus, some may be excluded voluntarily from the deliberative process. Hence, inclusion has its limits; we cannot include those who do not want to participate.

The main objection to forcing citizens to participate in deliberation is that this may contradict their idea of politics or even their idea of the good life. There may be groups for whom participating in deliberation would seem to be simply wrong. For example, a group of Trotskyists may believe that change has to come through revolution rather than through changing the system from the inside and that participating in political institutions rooted in a capitalist system is morally wrong. For them, participating in the deliberative process and especially accepting its values of mutual respect and tolerance towards other points of view, not to mention other-regarding behaviour towards capitalists, would count as a betrayal of their value system. We can say that Trotskyists and deliberative democrats have different conceptions of politics (Gaus 1999). Another example is the case of the Amish, who choose to withdraw both from society in general and from political participation in particular.

We can certainly tell people about the benefits of participation, but we cannot go further than this, when deliberation is not a value-neutral concept. It requires participants to interact with other groups in very specific ways, take on other-regarding attitudes and tolerate and respect other points of view. Thus we must accept voluntary exclusion, even if we feel that this will impoverish the political process by removing some voices from it.

However, some would argue that non-participation and political exclusion are rarely, if ever, voluntary (Barry 2002) and are brought about by the fact that the values and practices of groups and individuals are not recognized or respected by the majority, or because individuals or groups feel that they will not be able to affect the outcomes of the process and as a result withdraw from participation. This raises a dilemma for liberals. On the one hand they may want to respect the choice of individuals not to participate, yet on the other hand equality might not be ensured without making participation compulsory for all. Nonetheless, this does not diminish the force of the argument that democratic deliberation is not value-neutral and thus we should allow those who object to its values to refrain from participating. This illustrates that as all political systems are value-laden, they will always serve as a device of exclusion for those who reject their core values. The question is whether this will lead to the exclusion of the many or the few. Democracy, through its intrinsic values, does admirably well in excluding very few individuals.

The external inclusion of arguments

But it is not enough to ensure the inclusion of people in deliberative democracy. In order for it to fulfill its function and to provide reasoned and well-balanced debate, we also have to make sure that all relevant ideas, facts, beliefs and arguments will be included in deliberation. This is especially important if not all citizens can take part and we need to choose participants through random sampling or representation. And not only should every relevant argument be included in deliberation, but it should also be presented as competently as possible, in order to ensure that its inclusion is not purely a gesture. This is important not only for outcome-based justifications, but also for process-based ones, as there is procedural value in conducting a balanced discussion, since this implies that all members of society are included and respected.

The inclusion of all arguments is just as important for the theory of deliberative democracy as the inclusion of all individuals. The reason for this is that deliberation is not about the sheer numbers and distribution of preferences in society, but rather about reasoned arguments and reciprocity. Thus it focuses on listening to each other's arguments and transforming our preferences and making decisions based on them. If we define inclusion in this way, we can say that no individual is excluded from deliberation, as long as his or her arguments are presented as competently as possible.

Those who argue for multiculturalism (Kymlicka 1995) or a 'politics of presence' (Phillips 1995) may object that deliberation conceived in this way may allow all points of view to be presented by the most dominant group in society, such as white heterosexual males in Western democracies. This goes against arguments that the best way to represent women or minorities is to include them directly in the decision-making process instead of allowing others to represent their interests, however benevolent these representatives may be. Representation should thus be descriptive; each representative is a member of the social group he or she represents (Mansbridge 1999a).

However, note that this definition requires not only that each argument should be put forward during deliberative debate, but also that it should be put forward *as competently as possible*. It is most likely going to be a member of the group whose arguments and interests are being represented who can put these forward in the most competent way, although exceptions exist, of course, such as children or the mentally ill. It may be that men are able to put forward arguments in favour of women quite competently, just as Wilberforce was able to put forward arguments on behalf of black African slaves that eventually led to the abolition of slavery in Britain. However, it is likely that black African slaves would have been able to put these arguments forward even more competently as a result of shared lived experience, interests and beliefs. Thus descriptive representation will play a large role in deliberative politics as well.

This definition of democratic inclusion is in fact a useful counter against essentialism in identity politics. Not all women, blacks, Asians or Latinos have the same interests and hold the same beliefs (Phillips 1995; Young 2000). An equality of arguments is thus better than a system of quotas in representation. While I may not be certain that my interests will be accurately represented by a woman, if my arguments are put forward during deliberation at least as competently as I could have put them forward, this ensures that they will receive due consideration.

One idea for ensuring such an inclusion of arguments in practice has been put forward by Dryzek and Niemeyer (2008). Their theory of discursive representation envisages a chamber of discourses where each discourse is represented by someone who has been selected especially because they are able to do so competently. In order to achieve this, they propose a sampling technique that combines discourse analysis with Q methodology, a technique for analyzing subjective data in the social sciences. First, discourse analysis enables us to put together a list of statements that are representative of the major discourses in society about an issue. Second, Q methodology allows us to identify those members of a randomly selected sample whose beliefs best correspond to each of these discourses. Based on the assumption that these individuals are able to represent the discourses they believe in competently, they could then deliberate on our behalf in a chamber of discourses.

However, we can object to such a system on the grounds that deliberation should be accessible to all citizens. In the case of organizing political deliberation based on random sampling or jury duty, each relevant citizen would have an equal probability of being selected. In the case of descriptive representation deliberators would be selected based on their membership of certain groups in society. But this is not the case for the chamber of discourses, which favours citizens with strong, maybe even biased views.

One important qualification regarding the inclusion of arguments that deliberative democrats often make is that deliberation should include all *reasonable* members of society. The question then arises: what makes an argument unreasonable enough to exclude it?

Deliberative democracy cannot accommodate coercion and views that are hateful or threatening towards others. It cannot accommodate arguments that demand the violation of the basic rights of others or that blatantly discriminate against others based on gender, race or other characteristics. Such arguments should clearly be excluded from deliberation. All of them constitute straightforward cases of repulsive viewpoints: no one would want to see deliberative debate as an opportunity for aspiring slave-owners and others who hold repulsive preferences to publicize and promote their beliefs.

Other viewpoints, which are less obviously morally wrong, should, however, not be excluded from deliberation. Thus, the rules of deliberation need to allow some selfish viewpoints or arguments which are not universally accepted and may be hotly contested by a majority in society. As there cannot be an authority outside and above the deliberative process that would determine whether or not such arguments are 'acceptable' or 'reasonable', excluding them would undermine that process. An important reason for this is that the acceptability of many arguments changes over time; a hundred years ago homosexuality was not considered to be a publicly acceptable practice.

Young (2000) argues that the reasonableness of deliberative participants is less about the beliefs and preferences they hold than about their psychological attitudes, such as openness. Deliberation cannot accommodate those who are unwilling to listen to the arguments of others and adjust their own beliefs as a result: 'Since reasonable people often disagree about what proposals, actions, groundings, and narratives are rational or irrational, judging too quickly is itself often a symptom of unreasonableness' (Young 2000: 24). Such persons would not fulfill their deliberative obligations of other-regardingness and a willingness to transform beliefs and preferences. According to Young, reasonable people also enter deliberation with the intention of reaching an agreement, or in cases where deliberation is used as an exploratory tool, with the intention of understanding other points of view better and maybe approximating an agreement.

No deliberative democrat would argue that people with such unreasonable attitudes should be excluded. But it is not desirable to base a definition of reasonableness on attitudes and character traits, rather than beliefs and arguments. First, such traits can be subjective and difficult to measure. There are no ways in which we can define who is too stubborn to make a good deliberator. If deliberation works as deliberative democrats intended, such individuals would be punished by the process if a more other-regarding majority dominated it instead. Second, people can change. Deliberative democracy is meant to encourage people to become more open, other-regarding and tolerant (Gutmann and Thompson 1996). Thus, we cannot exclude anyone in advance. Finally, and most importantly, we cannot discriminate against people based on their personal characteristics, especially as all people will be stubborn and lack other-regarding attitudes at least some of the time. Thus, most of us would have to be labelled unreasonable occasionally if not frequently, no matter how reasonable a belief or position we hold.

Internal inclusion

Once the deliberative group is constituted, internal inclusion needs to be ensured. It is not enough to guarantee that all possible participants are present during deliberation. All deliberators should be equally included in the debate and no reasonable deliberator should be marginalized. It is perfectly possible to imagine a situation where all of those substantively affected have been invited, yet during the actual discussion some are marginalized while the views of others receive great attention. Once again, it is important that we pay attention to the inclusion of both people and ideas.

Even in small groups, people will take on different roles, such as the leader or the scapegoat (Levine and Moreland 1990). Studies of jury deliberations show that men talk more and have a greater influence on the outcome of the procedure than women (Hastie *et al.* 1983). Deliberative democrats need to develop credible mechanisms for levelling the playing field in the face of such tendencies.

According to difference democrats, deliberation can lead to internal exclusion. Young (2000) argues that deliberative norms entail dispassionate speech and that good argument is defined by standards laid down by white male elites. Those who are perceived to be governed by their passions rather than reason, use emotional language and hand gestures and in general do not conform to the standards of a seminar room are likely to be ignored. Different cultural groups communicate in ways which conform to these standards to varying degrees. As an example, people from Latin cultures are often louder and use more emotional language and expansive hand gestures. In addition, women are often seen to be more emotional than men. Those who are less articulate, struggle to express their thoughts or express their arguments in circuitous rather than logically straightforward ways are also going to be disadvantaged and are less likely to be listened to. The dominant group of white middle- and upper-class men have an advantage, having been educated to make logically well-structured arguments and to conform to standards of dispassionateness and articulateness.

As a result, Young (1996, 2000) proposes that deliberative democrats need to introduce other forms of communication in addition to logical reasoning and presents three of these: greeting or public acknowledgement, rhetoric and narrative. Her interpretation of deliberative democracy follows the Habermasian tradition in that it is based on speech act theory, but is differentiated from it by her focus on inequalities and social differences. In order to signal the communicative inclusiveness of her model, Young calls her conception of deliberative democracy 'communicative democracy'.

This model helps to reconcile the tensions between giving priority to the best argument and including all on an equal basis in deliberation, and thereby overcoming existing structural inequalities. However, such attempts will always be vulnerable to prioritizing inclusion over solid argumentation to the point where one of the key features of deliberative democracy is undermined. In the cacophony of plural cultural expressions the power of the best argument is severely diminished.

Greeting or public acknowledgment is about acknowledging each other as members of the group and committing ourselves to listening to each other and is thus crucial for inclusion. It is a conscious act of recognizing others' and our own irreducible particularity. The speaker signals that not only is he or she aware of the fact of others' existence, but also of the distance that separates them from each other in their lived experiences and perspectives.

Greetings also initiate relationships and invite responses from others and are thus crucial for building relationships between deliberators. Greeting can also signal a relationship of equality and help to establish trust, but it will not always do so. The importance of greeting is demonstrated by the fact that in politics, especially in international relations, its form is often ritualized.

Rhetoric allows deliberators to attempt to influence each other through figurative and emotive language. It allows for strength of feeling to be communicated. Following Habermas some deliberative democrats (Bohman 1988) differentiate between rational speech that makes assertions about the world and signals that the speaker is ready to defend those assertions, and rhetoric that aims to manipulate others rather than fostering understanding. Rational speech is dispassionate, logical and neutral and focuses on evidence and logical connections that support an argument. Rhetoric is often emotional and uses figurative language to engage the passions and the imagination of listeners. Young (2000) argues that rational speech is not in fact neutral, but reflects the style used by people occupying a particular social position. Furthermore, she argues that politics is never truly free of rhetoric. Thus we should focus on what the substance of an argument is, rather than on how that argument is made. Rhetoric is useful in political deliberation, because by engaging the passions it helps to put new issues on the agenda and it does not exclude those who do not communicate in the style of rational speech.

Narrative serves to introduce the perspectives of different members of the group on an issue and is also advocated by Sanders (1997), who calls it testimony. It gives voice to the experiences and viewpoints of different members of the community and is therefore key in including various social perspectives during deliberation. It does not rely on shared assumptions, but highlights the differences in assumptions between different members of society. It counters preconceived notions of how others in society live, helps people to find out why others hold certain values and is hence an important source of information. Without deliberation people know much about their own preferences and interests, but little about those of others (Nino 1996). Narratives allow us to find out why others hold the preferences they do. They also allow individuals who share a common perspective to build a shared identity and identify the basis of their affinity.

These three forms of communication – greeting, rhetoric and narrative – help to increase the internal inclusiveness of deliberative democracy, as their practice confers respect towards members of minority groups. However, even introducing these types of communication will not always ensure inclusion. Therefore more practical measures are needed that ensure that no one is left out of the debate.

One practical institutional measure that organizers of deliberative meetings adopt to foster internal inclusion is the use of trained moderators, as in Fishkin's deliberative polls. Moderators aim to ensure internal inclusion by making sure that all members of the group have opportunities to speak and feel comfortable about doing so. In order to achieve this, moderators need to make sure that no one is intimidated by others and that more assertive members of the group do not hijack the discussion.

In order for deliberation to function properly, one has to acknowledge the importance of small-talk. At the start of a meeting participants will normally greet each other and exchange a few words. This small-talk allows people to connect to each other. Young acknowledges that it is possible to exchange formal greetings with someone at the beginning of a meeting and then ignore that person afterwards (Young 2000: 61). Small-talk does not allow us to do this so easily, since it makes our fellow deliberators more human. Thus it could be important in micro deliberative meetings to introduce opportunities for such small-talk, such as coffee breaks and lunches. These would also allow deliberators to discuss the main issue of the day more informally, without the pressure of being seen to take a stand in public.

Requirements of civility (Rawls 1997; Estlund 2008; Bohman and Richardson 2009) can also affect the extent to which deliberators are included and excluded. Those who do not behave or talk in a civil manner during deliberation may exclude others by their actions or may find themselves excluded. Unreasonable beliefs or behaviour will cause problems for internal inclusion, just as they did for external inclusion.

It is only so far that such suggestions can go in ensuring internal inclusion. Even if we allow narratives and rhetoric in a deliberative debate, we cannot ensure that these will be taken seriously. Increased inclusion may undermine the reasoned debate that gives the best argument its power. While increasing inclusion is probably the most inspiring aim of deliberative democrats, they offer limited suggestions as to how such inclusion could be ensured in practice and there is no clear indication that deliberative democracy guarantees this value better than other models of democracy.

Equality

Formal equality

As I have argued at the beginning of this chapter, the legitimacy of deliberative procedures relies not only on inclusion, but also on equality. The first type of equality I will examine here is formal equality; the minimal levels of equality provided for all by the rules of the decision-making procedure.

Over the course of the twentieth century, citizens of liberal democracies have become equal in the formal sense. Each citizen can cast one vote in elections regardless of income, gender or race. Each citizen has a right to free speech and assembly, the right to contact their representatives, to participate in demonstrations and to run for office. Of course, not all citizens make equal use of these rights; many people do not vote in elections, most citizens never contact their representatives and even fewer citizens run for local office, let alone participate in national politics. Furthermore, there is substantial inequality between citizens when it comes to their ability to influence politics, for example through political activism or campaign financing.

Formal equality has also been the primary concern of democratic theorists. Minimal models of democracy are defined through the formal rights held by citizens. These include rights to freedom of speech and assembly, a right to participate in politics through periodic voting and standing for elected office (Dahl 1989). While these rights are important for deliberative democracy as well, they may need to be supplemented by others in order to account for the dialogic nature of deliberation.

Every member of a political community should have the right to participate in the deliberative process. Of course, it is open to interpretation how we define who counts as a member of a political community. At the very minimum this must include citizens of voting age, but as we have seen in Chapter 2, this could be extended to non-citizen residents of a country who are affected by the policy under discussion, or even those who have not yet reached the official voting age.

Ensuring both external and internal inclusion is the first step towards establishing formal equality among deliberators. In macro deliberation formal equality is ensured as long as citizens have a right to free speech and free assembly and have the right to participate in some form of public sphere deliberation. In micro models of deliberation this principle extends to the selection of deliberators. By making sure that all substantively affected individuals have an equal opportunity to participate, selecting deliberators through a procedure that allows everyone a fair chance to be chosen or by selecting deliberators in a way that ensures that each relevant point of view is represented competently, we give citizens a formally equal chance of influencing the outcome. The same applies to making sure that no participants of deliberation are marginalized or treated without respect. Thus, there is a very strong link between inclusion and formal equality. Furthermore, the rules regulating deliberation have to treat each participant in the same way (Cohen 1989). Thus all should be able to contribute to setting the agenda and all should be allowed to provide and request justifications for beliefs and preferences.

There are some aspects of deliberative procedures in which formal equality can be ensured relatively straightforwardly. If briefing materials are distributed before the deliberative debate, we can make sure that every deliberator receives these. If there is a vote at the end of the debate, formal equality can be ensured by giving each person a vote.

When it comes to the actual deliberative debate, we still have some, albeit more limited options for ensuring formal equality, by designing rules of order which make sure that all have a roughly equal share in participation. The most obvious way of doing this is by introducing a maximum speaking time for each participant. In *Deliberation Day*, Ackermann and Fishkin (2004) require that each deliberator should be given five minutes of floor time in their group. They set no minimal speaking requirements; deliberators are allowed to stay silent. Those who have exhausted their five-minute time limit can only speak again if no one else wishes to do so. If we want deliberation to be slightly more informal and strict time-keeping would get in the way of this, moderators can be used to ensure that individuals have roughly equal amounts of speaking time available to them.

Time constraints are likely to be a significant factor in limiting formal political equality in a deliberative democracy. As Dahl (2006: 57) notes:

As the number of citizens who wish to speak increases, the costs in time rise steeply. In a unit with just twenty citizens, if each citizen were allowed to speak for ten minutes, the meeting would require two hundred minutes, or more than three hours. In a unit with fifty citizens, to allow each citizen to speak for ten minutes would require a full eight hour day; in a unit of five hundred citizens, more than ten eight hour days! (Dahl 2006: 57)

It is unlikely that in a town of a thousand citizens everyone would have a say, let alone in a country the size of the United Kingdom. Ackermann and Fishkin (2004) get around this constraint by dividing citizens into small groups. However, as a result, each citizen's likelihood of having an impact on the outcome of the procedure becomes minuscule, just as it is in the case of voting. Thus, citizens either have to be included in deliberation indirectly, at the most having equal *opportunity to be selected* to participate or will have to see their influence severely diminished.

Imposing formal time constraints would also ensure that arguments are to the point. Difference democrats will surely cry foul at this, as arguments to the point will most likely lack rhetoric and emotional language. Those more skilled at public speaking and concise reasoning will be able to make much better use of the time allotted to them. Thus, such measures tell us little about the substantive equality of deliberators. Some may be able to use their five minutes of speaking time much more effectively than others.

Once maximum speaking times are set, similarly it might be beneficial to set a minimum speaking time as well. If someone has agreed to participate in a deliberative discussion, it would surely be best to ensure that he or she will actually contribute to the debate. Individuals might feel that they do not have much insight to give, but one of the main values of deliberation is exactly that everyone's opinions should be listened to with equal attention. And making everyone speak also ensures that they will give the issue some thought and thus contribute to a better outcome.

How about ensuring formal equality of arguments? This could be defined as a requirement that all relevant arguments should receive some equal, minimal consideration. While this could be achieved with the help of moderators and briefing documents, this is a more subjective assessment than that of whether each deliberator had an equal opportunity to take part in the debate.

Despite the problem of time constraints, some form of formal equality appears to be possible during micro deliberative meetings. Nonetheless, formal equality on its own is a relatively weak procedural value that is already satisfied by current liberal democracies. In order to justify deliberative democracy on the basis of equality, deliberative democrats need to focus on its ability to produce substantive equality.

Substantive equality

Rules that provide formal equality will not ensure that all members of a deliberative group are substantively equal. Despite formal equality in liberal representative democracies, those who are better educated and better off are often able to make better use of their rights, such as contacting their representatives or running for office. Endorsements by Hollywood celebrities can have an influence on political campaigns that ordinary people cannot replicate. At the much publicized extreme, the most powerful and wealthiest individuals and groups may be able to fund parties and politicians to an extent that the latter feel obliged to repay their generosity with policies that support them.

Research on group behaviour shows that status differences are common both in small and large groups. Those with high status are likely to behave differently both non-verbally, by standing straight and maintaining eye contact, and verbally, by speaking more often and interrupting others more often (Levine and Moreland 1990). Not only does high status alter the behaviour of those at the top, but this also translates into differences of actual power and influence. Those with a higher social status outside the deliberative group are likely to be more powerful within the deliberative group. In the absence of substantive equality, their arguments will carry more weight and they will have more influence on the final decisions.

This is largely due to an inequality in the allocation of resources, such as time, social status, wealth, connections or knowledge. The resources that are relevant in deliberation are mostly positional goods that only become meaningful through interactions with others. Our social status is dependent on our position within society, and money and wealth are only useful if there are others who are willing to trade their goods for our cash.

Deliberative democrats recognize the need for substantive equality in order to make democratic deliberation legitimate. However, they disagree over the way in which such substantive equality should be conceptualized. Theorists writing on this question usually approach it from the perspective of contemporary theories of justice. One of the key debates in this field is defining the domain over which individuals are equal in a just society. While these theorists have similar concerns to those of difference democrats, they use a different set of concepts to solve the problems of inclusion and equality.

The first way of answering the 'equality of what?' question is by turning to Rawls's (1972) concept of primary goods. These are the characteristics of institutions and society that are necessary in order to establish a just society and which enable each rational human being to pursue his or her conception of the good. These include the social bases of self-respect, basic rights and liberties, freedom of movement and occupation, as well as the income and basic goods necessary for survival.

The second answer in the literature is to base substantive equality on Sen's capabilities approach (1992). For Sen, living consists of a variety of functionings, such as being well-nourished, being happy or having self-respect. The more functionings we are capable of performing, or in other words, the larger our capability set is, the more free we are to choose from possible livings (Sen 1992: 40). Thus a person's well-being and freedom are linked to the range of functionings that he is capable of effectively choosing from. This approach focuses not only on the resources available to individuals, but also on their ability to convert those resources into successfully realized lives, whatever their personal characteristics or their conception of the good life may be. This reflects the fact that someone who is disabled, for example, may need more of a resource such as money than a healthy person in order to achieve the same level of functioning. Similarly, different conceptions of the good will require different amounts of resources.

Bohman (1997) has adopted Sen's capabilities approach in his analysis of inequality in deliberation. He argues that equality of opportunities, resources and capabilities is needed to ensure effective social freedom and through it democratic legitimacy. His analysis centres on the capacities citizens have to influence deliberation. Citizens need to possess a range of relevant capabilities in order to be able to participate in deliberation. Bohman argues that the most important of these is the ability to initiate debate, but they could also include cognitive capacities and the ability to communicate effectively.

Furthermore, members of a community should also be able to challenge prevailing norms of deliberation and reasoning. This echoes the concerns of difference democrats, especially Young, and ensures that deliberative capabilities are not defined rigidly, so as to be exclusive. Bohman calls the lack of developed public capacities political poverty and argues that just like economic poverty, it is also subject to a poverty trap.

Knight and Johnson (1997) argue that the kind of equality we should be looking for in a deliberative democracy is equal opportunity of access to political influence. For this they borrow Dworkin's (1987) definition of political impact and political influence. Political impact is the change that any one individual can effect, such as the vote that each citizen holds. Political influence, on the other hand, is the extent to which each individual can make his views heard and influence others to agree with him. Knight and Johnson state that equal outcomes should never be the aim of democracy, because uncertainty of outcomes is an essential part of democratic decision making. They also choose to equalize capabilities, rather than resources, to achieve political equality. They define politically relevant capabilities as the ability to formulate authentic preferences, the ability to use cultural resources effectively and basic cognitive abilities and skills.

Thus the literature favours equalizing capabilities over equalizing primary goods (Peter 2007b). The reason for this is that the capabilities approach offers us a better perspective on how far deliberators would be able to use their resources to succeed, instead of focusing simply on the existence of those resources, as the primary goods approach does. Moreover, in the political context there exists a definite range of capabilities that are necessary for successful participation. Given the plurality of conceptions of the good, no equivalent way of assessing capability sets exists in a more general context of living (Cohen 1995).

However, it is very likely that such substantive equality of capabilities will not exist in deliberative debates. While it is possible to eliminate the most egregious inequalities, such as lack of food, shelter or other basic necessities, equalizing capabilities for the much higher level of human functioning that deliberation requires is not so easy. We can define a minimal level of capabilities that all citizens should possess, but beyond that there is still going to be a large degree of variation in the extent to which individuals can successfully participate in and influence deliberation. The extent of these is likely to be such that significant levels of substantive inequality will continue to exist even in deliberative democracies.

Part of the reason for this is that these inequalities are not only social – stemming from inequalities and injustices in society – but also natural – stemming from the natural abilities of individuals. These include our talents, our strengths and weaknesses. Many abilities, such as the ability to play the piano well or having green fingers, will be entirely irrelevant for deliberation, of course. But many others will have a significant impact on how likely individuals will be able to formulate an argument that stands up in deliberation and how likely that argument will impact the thinking of other group members. Not everyone possesses the rhetorical talents of Cicero. Shy individuals might find it hard to introduce an argument at all. Arguments presented more forcefully might have a bigger impact, regardless of their merit on their own. Civic education might help to reduce some of these inequalities in ability, but it will not eradicate them.

Inequalities in resources and abilities cannot be easily remedied through the procedural rules of deliberative democracy. Moreover, one can also make the stronger claim that substantive equality as a background condition of deliberative democracy is not only impossible, but also *undesirable*. To make deliberative democracy equal, in the sense that each group member is equally able to participate in deliberative discussions fruitfully, requires a redistribution of resources. But surely such redistribution cannot be imposed from the outside, but has to be arrived at through democratic institutions. Thus remedying inequalities over capabilities *before* deliberation would remove from the political forum important decisions about social justice and the way in which society should be organized (Peter 2007b).

There is likely to be reasonable disagreement in society over issues such as social justice, income distribution, education and so forth. Therefore, in a democratic polity these issues need to be decided through the political system. In the case of deliberative democracy, this would mean to a large extent through deliberative debate. If we pre-suppose that a 'correct' way of organizing society, distributing income and educating citizens exists, which will ensure an equality of capabilities that leads to political equality, these issues can no longer be subject to serious deliberation. However, under conditions of reasonable disagreement, this cannot legitimately be the case. Therefore, questions of social justice and redistribution need to remain the subject and possible outcome of deliberation, rather than one of its preconditions, no matter how unequal or imperfect this process may be. Citizens and representatives spend most of their time outside a deliberative setting and therefore it is not enough to demand that something is desirable in deliberation – it has to be shown that it is desirable outside of deliberation as well.

Furthermore, we need to remember that deliberation is about reasons and arguments, not just persons. Thus there is a limit to the extent that it is necessary for deliberators to be equal. Jane Mansbridge argues that equality in deliberation does not require equal influence. For 'the force of the better argument ... should prevail, no matter from whom that argument originates or how frequently it originates from one or more participants' (Mansbridge 1999b: 225). Thus it does not matter if some members of the group only infrequently influence the outcome, because this influence should belong to those with the better arguments. But this line of reasoning could still fall prey to substantive inequality, as it assumes that the better argument will prevail. The best arguments might belong to those group members who are not listened to, who are marginalized, who cannot articulate their thoughts well enough or who are bad at presenting themselves.

Finally, let us turn briefly to the idea that substantive equality should be extended to ideas and arguments as well. This clearly cannot be the case. Deliberative democracy requires that the best argument should be favoured. Even though equal respect for all is a fundamental tenet of deliberative democracy, it is hard to see how deliberators could or should respect everyone's arguments equally. Some arguments will necessarily be better than others, and nothing is gained by demanding that each of these should be treated equally. A minimal condition of formal equality can be posited, asserting that each relevant argument should be included and presented as compe-tently as possible and a minimal amount of time and resources should be allocated to each relevant argument. However, it would not profit deliberative democrats to argue for more than this.

Conclusion

We can now summarize the above arguments about equality and inclusion in deliberation (see also Table 4.1). The most valuable aspect of deliberative procedures is that they strive towards inclusion. As a result, deliberative democrats address possible solutions to an important procedural value, which is often neglected in the practice of democratic decision making, even if not in its theory. However, it is not clear how deliberative mechanisms can guarantee the external and internal inclusion of people and arguments better than other models of democracy. This makes inclusion a theoretically desirable, but a practically problematic value for deliberation. Furthermore, deliberative democrats are not unique in recognizing the need for political inclusion and their solution to it is not necessarily the strongest available. Thus while this focus on inclusion is admirable, it does not necessarily make deliberative democracy better than other models of democracy.

Table 4.1 An overview of types of equality and inclusion

	PEOPLE	ARGUMENTS
FORMAL EQUALITY	All those affected should have equal minimal rights/opportunity to participate. Desirable.	All relevant arguments receive some equal minimal consideration. Desirable.
SUBSTANTIVE EQUALITY	All those affected should be equally capable of participating competently in deliberation. Impossible and possibly undesirable.	Equal resources/capabilities should be devoted to each argument. Undesirable.
EXTERNAL INCLUSION	All those affected should be included in the deliberative process either directly or through representative mechanisms. Desirable but problematic.	All relevant arguments are represented. Desirable but problematic.
INTERNAL INCLUSION	No participants should be excluded or marginalized during the actual discussion. Desirable but problematic.	All relevant arguments are represented. Desirable but problematic.

Equality causes even more problems for deliberative democracy. We can define and enforce formal equality during deliberation, for example by providing each deliberator with an equal amount of speaking time. While this is a relatively weak procedural value that does not offer any advances over aggregative and minimal models of democracy, it is still desirable and it is the easiest to guarantee of the different variations of inclusion and equality that I have examined in this chapter.

Achieving substantive equality in deliberation is a much more ambitious aim, but one that it is necessary to aspire to, given that the outcomes of deliberation are more susceptible to differences in influence than the outcomes of voting. Thus it is important to try to equalize the capabilities of individuals to participate successfully in deliberative debates. However, substantive equality is difficult to achieve, since it would require not only wide-ranging social changes, but also an equalization of individual abilities to argue persuasively. Furthermore, it may even be undesirable to require substantive equality as a precondition of democratic deliberation, since this would require the widescale development of policies through the democratic process itself in order to be legitimate.

5
Deliberation and Decision Making

Compared to other models of democracy, the theory of deliberative democracy places relatively little emphasis on the actual moment of decision making. However, all forms of democracy will have to deliver decisions in a timely and non-arbitrary manner. This chapter discusses how deliberative forms of democracy can do this.

First, the chapter examines the model of democracy that focuses most on the actual moment of decision making through voting: aggregative democracy, which takes voting or other methods of counting individual preferences as the central moment of the democratic process. Deliberative democrats often argue expressly against this view of democracy, thus it is important to examine what the model they set themselves up against looks like. This may seem like a strange detour, because the approach of social choice theorists appears so different from that of deliberative democrats. However, this is misleading, as theorists of both persuasions have argued for democratic deliberation and their work can be complementary (Dryzek and List 2003; Goodin 2003; List 2004). Furthermore, both approaches fall under the broader heading of contemporary democratic theory and therefore it pays to understand social choice theory in order to make a full evaluation of the theory of deliberative democracy.

Next, we look at the possibility and normative importance of consensus for deliberative democrats and the alternative strategies that can be adopted if a unanimous decision proves to be impossible or undesirable. This means that deliberation will need to be combined with other forms of democratic decision making. We examine two of these in detail. Voting, either in elections or referendums, is the most obvious way in which deliberative democracy can make decisions. But deliberation could also be combined with bargaining in order to craft a compromise acceptable to all parties.

Aggregative and Deliberative Models of Democracy

The problem with voting

One strong theme in the deliberative democracy literature is that deliberation is a response to aggregative conceptions of democracy which take voting, elections and referendums to be the essence of politics. According to this model, democratic decision making works through collecting the preferences of all relevant individuals and using a rule to make a decision based on them. To put it more formally, aggregative models of democracy and social choice theory focus on the ways in which individual preferences are turned into social outputs or choices.

Most of the time, of course, we would conceive of such a mechanism as voting, but this need not always be the case. In fact, we could have a rule whereby decisions are always made by a dictator or a small group of oligarchs. Decisions might be made by lottery as well. Most commonly, the result of an aggregation rule is a social preference ordering, or in other words, the way in which citizens collectively rank available options.

These preferences are assumed to possess certain basic characteristics. The first of these is the most technical one: preferences need to be *reflexive,* meaning that each alternative x is weakly preferred to itself (that is, an agent is indifferent between x and itself). The other characteristics are more intuitive. Preferences need to be *complete,* that is, individuals have to be capable of comparing any two alternatives; formally, for any two alternatives x and y, either x is weakly preferred to y or y is weakly preferred to x (or both). Finally, preferences need to be *transitive*: if an individual weakly prefers x over y and y over z, she will also weakly prefer x over z.

However, according to findings in social choice theory, results reached through such a procedure can suffer from problems of *instability, impossibility* and *ambiguity* (Riker 1982). This has been most comprehensively proven by Arrow's impossibility theorem (Arrow 1951) and could pose fundamental problems for the legitimacy of democratic decision making. If the results of democratic voting are unstable and ambiguous, how can we take them to be any kind of representation of the collective will? In order to see whether this charge holds, let us examine the problem in more detail.

Instability

The problem of cycling was first observed in the eighteenth century by Condorcet in his famous paradox (1994). The paradox consists of the fact that pair-wise majority voting can result in a collective preference relation such as $x > y > z > x$, where $>$ stands for 'is strictly preferred to'. In these situations there is no clear winner, as each of the options will be defeated by another in pair-wise majority voting. This makes voting results *unstable*. And instability in turn opens up opportunities for strategic voting and manipulation:

	First choice	*Second choice*	*Third choice*
Anna	Friday	Saturday	Sunday
Bob	Saturday	Sunday	Friday
Clive	Sunday	Friday	Saturday

Let us illustrate the problem with a simple example. Three people – Anna, Bob and Clive – need to decide when to meet up for dinner. A majority (Anna and Clive) prefer Friday to Saturday and Saturday to Sunday (Anna and Bob). Yet, should Friday be proposed as the meeting day, this would be defeated by a majority (Bob and Clive) that prefers Sunday to Friday. But Saturday is still preferred by Anna and Bob to Sunday, which is in turn worse than Friday for Anna and Clive. And so on. Thus, whatever option is proposed, a majority will always be able to defeat the proposal. Knowing everyone else's preferences, Clive could pretend that his first choice is Friday and a decision could be made, but this act of manipulation will leave Bob badly off.

Impossibility

The second problem is that of *impossibility*. This is at the heart of Arrow's theorem (Arrow 1951/1963), which states that there is no aggregation rule which satisfies a few seemingly innocuous conditions. These conditions are:

- *universal domain*: all logically possible preference orderings are allowed in voting;

- *ordering of preferences*: the aggregation rule produces a reflexive, complete and transitive preference ordering;
- *weak Pareto principle*: if all individuals prefer x to y then society also prefers x to y;
- *non-dictatorship*: social preference orderings are not determined by an individual dictator; and
- *independence of irrelevant alternatives*: the social preference over x and y depends only on the individual preferences over x and y and not on preferences over other alternatives.

Independence of irrelevant alternatives can be explained with a simple example. If I am trying to make a choice between an apple and a banana, the introduction of a third option, say a clementine, should not influence my preference ordering over the original options. Put even more simply, if between an apple and a banana I would choose the apple, should you offer me a clementine as a new, third option, I should not then change my mind and opt for the banana. This may seem straightforward, but there are voting rules which do violate this condition.

These conditions are regarded as necessary for achieving a fair and democratic outcome. Some of them, such as independence of irrelevant alternatives, are more technical in nature. Others, such as non-dictatorship, have an immediately obvious normative relevance to democratic legitimacy.

There are ways to overcome Arrow's impossibility theorem. By relaxing or dropping one or more of his original conditions, it is possible to find aggregation rules which satisfy the other conditions. If we restrict the number of choices available to two, we no longer face an impossibility theorem. May's theorem (1952) shows that for two options majority rule will satisfy a set of conditions that are very similar to those set out by Arrow. However, this assumes that the number of options can uncontroversially be reduced to two.

The condition that could be restricted most easily is universal domain, which ensures that no preference orderings can be ruled out in advance. By assuming that most of the population will not hold counter-intuitive preference orderings, such as ranking the far right party first, the far left party second and the centrist party third, we can find a possible escape route from the impossibility theorem. An example of such restriction of individual preferences is *single-peakedness*, which I will describe later on in this chapter.

The impossibility theorem could also be avoided by abandoning non-dictatorship. If we allow a dictator to make all our decisions for us, we can satisfy all of Arrow's other conditions. However, as this effectively means we are abandoning democracy, this route should not be pursued.

Ambiguity

But these escape routes do not solve the problem that using different aggregation procedures with the same set of inputs does not always lead to the same output (Riker 1982). The output is instead dependent on the aggregation or voting rule employed. As there are a large number of aggregation rules, even leaving aside dictatorships and oligarchies, it comes as no great surprise that they sometimes produce different results. While the Condorcet winner in pair-wise majority voting might be x, the Borda rule could declare y the winner using the same individual preferences as inputs. There is no single result and this leads to the *ambiguity* of democratic decisions. After all, when two different ways of counting votes result in different winners, how can we be sure that the decision is the right one?

The deliberative response

Deliberative democrats criticize aggregative models of democracy for conceptualizing politics as a problem of making a fair decision based on the distribution of preferences among the electorate, rather than a process through which citizens can make a reasoned decision that takes into account the relevant facts as well as the beliefs and interests of others. For them, the political arena is not primarily the scene of preference aggregation, but of preference formation and transformation. Accordingly, they hold that rather than seeking a reasoned agreement or consensus, aggregative models use brute mechanisms to calculate what the most acceptable decision is, without taking into account that if they are exposed to new facts and different points of view, citizens may choose differently from how they do on their own. And thus it could be argued that it is primarily this lack of reason and information that leads to some of the perverse results of social choice theory.

Deliberative democracy, then, is meant to be a corrective for the instability, impossibility and ambiguity of aggregative democracy. Discussions, mutual understanding and consensus are meant to ensure that results are more stable and less arbitrary. The most obvious way this can be achieved is through a unanimous or near-unanimous consensus over one of the options available. Such a consensus is seen as valuable because it is a decision reached through agreement in society, and not just a decision that is the result of counting votes or of power politics. Aiming for a consensus also shows a deep commitment on the part of participants to make legitimate decisions as part of a deliberative political community (Cohen 1996).

Consensus can be defined as agreement over a unique solution that is preferred most by every member of the group. A deep consensus will extend to the reasons for a decision and not just the decision itself. In deliberation consensus is reached through rational argument and mutual understanding of each other's perspectives. This relates to the notion of communicative rationality, discussed in Chapter 3, where agents are motivated to find solutions to problems through discourse.

This is the view of consensus that Habermas promotes. While definitions of consensus in the deliberative democracy literature are in general under-specified, his is the most developed one (1996a: 16–7). He differentiates between types of consensus depending on the issues at stake. Firstly, pragmatic discourses outline the possible options and their outcomes, subject to the information available to deliberators. They do not operate on the level of values. They simply state the different actions the group could take and their most likely effects. Only in rare cases will a consensus be formed based on pragmatic discourse, as different options will be favoured by different value systems. Deliberation will have to penetrate deeper than the simple level of options available and their likely outcomes and a consensus will need to be formed on the level of underlying values. Therefore, what is at stake is what Elster (1998) calls underlying preferences. These are preferences over different values or long-term goals rather than individual actions or policies.

Habermas divides this deeper consensus into two further categories: that of moral and ethical consensus. Moral consensus deals with issues which can be generalized for the whole of mankind and should be subject to the principle of universalization. Habermas (1996a: 165) cites 'questions of social policy, of tax law, or the organisation of educational and health-care systems, where the distribution of social wealth, life opportunities, and chances for survival in general are at stake' as cases where a moral consensus is necessary.

Ethical consensus is concerned with issues which are based on the interests and cultural context of a specific society, such as 'ecological questions concerning the protection of the environment and animals, questions of traffic control and city planning' (Habermas 1996a: 165).

One criticism of Habermas's definition of consensus is that the distinction between moral and ethical consensus is often unclear. Why is environmental protection an ethical issue and not a moral one, for example (Pellizzoni 2001)? Similarly, immigration control, another issue which Habermas classifies as ethical, has clear implications for 'survival in general', and thus has a moral dimension too. Health policies, which he takes to be moral issues, will also have ethical dimensions that may not be applicable to all societies at all times. Therefore it would be more accurate to say that such issues have both moral and ethical dimensions and any consensus reached will have to have appropriate moral and ethical components. A sharp distinction between the two types of consensus is then unnecessary.

Should a consensus be unavailable as different values and interests clash in deliberation, a compromise must be reached instead. Habermas, however, defines compromise in a way which attempts to regulate bargaining and neutralize bargaining power. Compromise needs to fulfill three conditions. It must be 'more advantageous to all than no arrangement whatever' (Habermas 1996a: 166), it must exclude those who withdraw from cooperation, and it must not allow the exploitation of one party by the other. Thus compromise can also be agreed to by everyone, albeit for different reasons. In this way the application of the discourse principle limits the extent to which bargaining power can be exercised.

The Problem with Consensus

Such a unified view of agreement presents significant problems in today's complex democratic societies (Bohman 1996; Young 2000). These societies are characterized by pluralism (Cohen 1996). There is no single overarching ethical or moral framework that all citizens subscribe to. Rather, there are a large number of different reasonable worldviews, many of which feature basic assumptions that are not commensurable with each other. Barber argues that in most societies consensual democracy cannot be genuinely political as it wills away conflict (Barber 1984: 150). Consensus in this case is either imposed or reflects the fact that intractable conflicts are avoided in political discussions. In plural societies, seeking a consensual decision can lead to a lack of solution for just about every political problem. A unique consensus is more likely to emerge in societies where members have a strong shared identity, that is, citizens share values and traditions that give them a sense of commonality. Furthermore, deep pluralism exists not just at the level of policy outcomes, but also at the level of basic values. Thus, even if various groups all support a policy, they could do so for very different reasons.

Deliberation might actually increase dissent as it becomes clear to deliberators just how strongly they feel about an issue or how different a problem's solutions are from each other (Knight and Johnson 1994). There might be instances when deliberators will realize that an issue which they have not given much thought to beforehand has an obvious solution. But if deliberation is to be meaningful, it will often be concerned with deeply divisive issues. It is quite conceivable that when they look at their underlying preferences, deliberators' beliefs in the rightness of their preferred options will become stronger.

But it is certainly not desirable that such divisive issues should be avoided simply in order to create an illusion of consensus (Johnson 1998). Furthermore, in politics, it is highly unlikely that these issues can be avoided at all. There are virtually no truly value-free decisions. Even the choice of pizza toppings can be subject to moral consideration if a group includes vegetarians, Muslims, Jews or Hindus.

A consensus could also mask problems of conformity or informational cascades (Sunstein 2003; see Chapter 3). Conformity can develop because of informal social pressures within the group or more widely within society. Informational cascades develop when one individual chooses to update his beliefs based on the fact that someone else who appears to be knowledgeable holds a certain belief, when that belief might in fact be incorrect. This in turn can cause another individual to update his beliefs as well. A critical mass of individuals can soon develop who hold beliefs not based on their own private information but based on the assumption that if others believe something, it must be true. One of the biggest dangers of informational cascades is that individuals fail to reveal their private information, and thus members of the group will not realize that they are in effect holding a false belief.

Thus, the fact that some group members express judgements different from those of the majority without any negative consequences for their dissent is an indicator of a healthy debate without coercion and pressures to conform.

Under conditions of plurality, a lack of consensus need not be a normative problem. Cohen's (1989) condition of consensual outcomes in ideal deliberation allows for decisions to be made through voting, as long as deliberators show a commitment to consensual decision making under the constraints of plurality. And after all, political theorists have long acknowledged the demanding nature of unanimous decision making. Locke (1988), writing in the late seventeenth century, allows for majority rule due to this reason. He writes:

> For if the consent of the majority shall not in reason, be received, as the act of the whole, and conclude every individual; nothing but the consent of every individual can make any thing to be the act of the whole: But such a consent is next impossible ever to be had, if we consider the Infirmities of Health, and Avocation of Business, which in a number, though much less than that of a Common-wealth, will necessarily keep many away from the publick Assembly. To which if we add the variety of Opinions and contra-riety of Interests, which unavoidably happen in all Collections of Men, the coming into Society upon such terms would be only like Catos' coming into the Theatre, only to go out again. (Locke 1988: 332–3)

Nearly a hundred years later Rousseau (1997), who is famously demanding in his advocacy of the general will, acknowledges that such a general will does not exist for all issues, as when it is absent decisions can be made based on partial interests instead. Finally, Rawls argues that the ideal of public reason is sustained even if a vote has to be held in case of disagreement (1997: 115).

Consensus Relaxed

There is a practical need to relax consensus and no normative reason against it. The first response to pluralistic cultural complexity is to confine consensual outcomes to the realm of political ideals. We can then admit that real plural societies will not live up to this ideal, while asserting that they should nevertheless aspire to it. Thus at the same time reality is acknowledged and the theoretical ideal of consensus is salvaged. But deliberative democrats could also relax the definition of consensus to one that they can credibly aspire to in the real world.

This has been done in three broad ways. First, at the level of content, by allowing for reasoned compromise or agreement on conclusions where no agreement can be found on the underlying moral or ethical premises. Here, consensus is defined less strictly in order to allow for the co-existence of different frameworks of inter-pretation. Second, consensus may be found not at the level of the individual decision, but at the level of an overarching framework within which we can think about decisions. Third, it can be argued that the normative demand for consensus in deliberative democracy concerns consensus over the procedure itself, rather than the content of the decisions it generates. According to this third formulation, consensus serves to legitimate democratic decision making.

Content-based solutions

Instead of a unique consensus some theorists introduce weaker concepts of agreement that attempt to accommodate multiple world-views within a society. Relaxing stronger definitions of consensus is justified in the literature not only on practical grounds. Difference democrats argue that seeking a strong, unique consensus may in many situations be harmful. According to Young (2000: 43), seeking a unique consensus or a common interest can serve as a vehicle for exclusion. Less privileged members of society might be asked to make sacrifices for a common good from which they would not receive any benefits. She argues that rather than seeking to find consensual agree-ments based on consensual reasons, the aim of deliberation should be to find workable solutions and arrive at particular judgements for well-defined problems (Young 2000: 29).

Habermas's way of relaxing consensus by accepting a compromise has already been described. While it allows for different reasons for a conclusion, this definition of compromise does not violate the spirit of deliberative democracy by regulating bargaining in order to make the procedure more equitable to all.

One of the most well-known ways of relaxing consensus is Rawls's concept of overlapping consensus (1987, 1993). He was not writing specifically in the context of deliberative democracy, but his concept has been used by others to underpin deliberation. Rawls argues that citizens can retain their comprehensive doctrines or frameworks which they use to explain the world, but as long as these doctrines are reasonable they should be able to arrive at a conception of justice in the political sphere that is acceptable to all. Thus he argues that an overlapping consensus is a political arrangement which can be accepted by all citizens holding reasonable comprehensive doctrines as they recognize that such a consensus is politically necessary. It is not a requirement, however, that citizens should start out by agreeing to an overlapping consensus. Over very long periods of time what was originally a *modus vivendi*, such as religious toleration, can become a constitutional consensus, that is a framework everyone is willing to live with, and eventually this will develop into an overlapping consensus once citizens recognize that it complements their comprehensive doctrine or, if it does not complement it, they are willing to redefine that doctrine. This last requirement makes it stronger than just a Habermasian compromise, which does not have such a reflexive quality.

Sunstein's (1994) incompletely theorized agreement is one of the most well-defined conditions for agreement without a unique consensus. While people are often able to agree on a course of action, under conditions of deep pluralism they may not be able to do so on the underlying reasons for it. Incompletely theorized agreements allow individuals to agree on a decision for very different reasons, without having to agree on those reasons as well. If there is agreement on a decision, then agreement on underlying reasons becomes practically unnecessary, is often infeasible to reach and can even be undesirable if it would lead to further divisions (List 2006). This places no demand on decision-makers to abandon their fundamental preferences, or in other words their worldview. It allows for the formation of unlikely coalitions as long as all members can agree on their preferred outcome. Deliberation can then be defined as a procedure which allows deliberators to try and convince each other of the best solution, while leaving their underlying preferences intact. Both of these ways of relaxing consensus require an agreement on outcomes, while allowing each decision-maker to come to this conclusion for different reasons, just as a Habermasian compromise does. The three theories thus have a lot in common.

Bohman (1996) criticizes Habermas and Rawls for the use of what he calls singular reason, where reasonable or consensual policies are articulated from only one perspective. He also disputes the fact that such singular reason should lead to consensual agreement. According to Bohman, 'plural agreement merely requires continued cooperation in public deliberation, even with persistent disagreements'.

Thus he introduces the concept of moral compromise. Moral compromises are frameworks that allow individuals to accommodate the values of others without necessarily having to give up their own. They develop as a result of discussion, as both sides change their framework of interpretation in a way that allows them to recognize each other's moral values. The aim is not to develop a consensus, but to allow the representation of both sides and ensure that neither will withdraw from the debate. Moral compromise should be both pluralistic and dynamic.

What all of the above ways of relaxing consensus have in common is agreement on the conclusion while permitting disagreement on the premises. But deliberation needs to function and arrive at decisions when not even a content-based consensus is available. Therefore we need to look at ways in which the definition of consensus can be further relaxed.

Meta-agreement

Even if substantive agreement cannot be reached over specific options, deliberation should help the group to define what the relevant dimensions are that they disagree over and what the most important issue dimension is (List 2004). Citizens often do not hold well-reasoned positions and clear preference orderings over issues, but participating in deliberation may help them to achieve this (Benhabib 1996). Quasi-experiments in deliberative polling seem to confirm the hypothesis that deliberative discussion increases preference structuration (Fishkin *et al.* 2007; Farrar *et al.* 2010), that is, more individuals tend to order their preferences along the same structuring dimension. The classic examples for such structuring dimensions include the left–right continuum in politics and the 'guns and butter' two-dimensional space, where 'guns' stand for defence spending and 'butter' stands for economic spending. Thus deliberation followed by voting has a procedural advantage over voting alone, as it ensures that most voters will evaluate issues according to the same parameters.

Meta-agreement can be the result of becoming better informed about issues during deliberation (Farrar *et al.* 2010). As the nature of the issues becomes clearer to individuals they might change their preference ordering based on new information in order to make it more compatible with underlying issue dimensions. They might also change their mind about the relative importance of issue dimensions.

The importance of deliberation might then become that it facilitates the development of single-peaked preference orderings across a group, and as a consequence makes it more likely that a mutually acceptable or at least representative outcome is found. Meta-agreement in fact corresponds to the concept of single-peakedness first defined by Duncan Black (1948). This is a characteristic of deliberation that is firmly based on an instrumental view of rationality and yet contributes to the justification of deliberative democracy by arguing that reasoned debate will lead to citizens forming new preferences and transforming old ones in a way that will help us to arrive at better decisions.

In order to understand the importance of single-peakedness, first we need to look at the social choice-theoretic problem of cycling. As we saw earlier, voting cycles were first discussed by Condorcet and refer to situations in which aggregating individual preference orderings – typically by majority voting – will result in a social ordering of $x > y > z > x$, where $>$ stands for 'is strictly preferred to'. In a case like this it is not clear which one is the winning alternative. The theoretical probability that cycles will occur increases as the number of voters and the number of available alternatives increases (Gehrlein 2002).

A sufficient, but not necessary condition for avoiding cycles, identified by Duncan Black (1948), is the presence of single-peakedness. Preferences are called *single-peaked* if the options can be arranged along a structuring dimension from left to right such that each individual has a most preferred option, and her preference over all other options decreases with increasing distance from the most preferred option. Accordingly, if there are three options (x, y and z) arranged in this order along a dimension, then an individual's preference ordering can take the form $x > y > z$, but cannot take the form $x > z > y$. The name 'single-peaked preferences' derives from the fact that in a diagram all lines have one single, clearly identifiable peak (see Figure 5.1). It is not essential to achieve perfect single-peakedness. With the increase of the proportion of single-peaked preference orderings in a group, the likelihood that cycles will appear will be reduced (Niemi 1969).

This would solve the problem of instability that Arrow's theorem

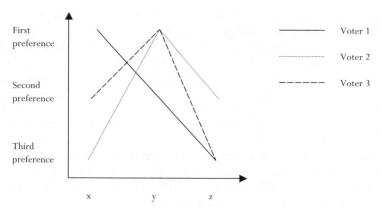

Figure 5.1   Single peaked preference orderings

implies for voting. In fact, this is a restriction of the condition of universal domain in the theorem. If preferences are structured along a few common dimensions, we would no longer be allowing all possible preference orderings, as the condition of universal domain demands. Thus deliberation could reduce the indeterminacy of voting outcomes to an extent where it poses negligible consequences.

If deliberation does increase the proportion of single-peaked preferences in the group, this will mean that it will achieve its objective of increasing the stability and coherence of decisions by creating the structural preconditions of agreement. However, some of the most persistent disagreements occur precisely when such a structuring dimension cannot be found. For those disagreements, meta-consensus will be of little help. And even if we locate a common issue dimension we still have not made an actual decision.

Procedure-based solutions

But maybe what the spirit of deliberation truly demands is not consensus over the content of decisions at all. Rather what we should be looking for is a consensus over the procedure of deliberation itself: all or nearly all citizens accepting it as the best and fairest way of arriving at a collective decision. Thus, for Gutmann and Thompson (1996) deliberative democracy is a procedure which has better chances of arriving at justifiable policies in the face of moral disagreements than other procedures.

According to Benhabib (1996: 73), 'agreements in societies living with value-pluralism are to be sought for not at the level of substantive beliefs but at that of procedures, processes, and practices for attaining and revising beliefs'. Thus, citizens need to agree that deliberation is the best way to reach decisions while at times they might disagree with those decisions. Therefore for Benhabib the concept of consensus is linked to legitimacy. Deliberative consensus is an agreement that legitimates deliberative democracy. This entails a consensus that every individual is entitled to self-respect and that deliberation should be based on rational argumentation which is interpreted in an other-regarding manner by listeners.

For Barber (1984) the task of politics is also legitimation. For him the political process can have three results. First, it can create a decision through bargaining and exchange. Second, it can reveal an already existing consensus. Third, it can transform conflict through a 'participatory process of ongoing, proximate self-legislation and the creation of a political community capable of transforming dependent private individuals into free citizens and partial and private interest into public goods' (Barber 1984: 151). It is through this third result that deliberation provides political legitimacy. As for Benhabib, this is a reflexive 'never-ending process of deliberation, decision and action' (Barber 1984: 151). What is crucial for a deliberative process is not ordinary consensus, but consensus over the legitimacy of this reflexive process.

What legitimates deliberative democracy for these authors is an agreement on an other-regarding, inclusive, reflexive procedure, which, as Gutmann and Thompson (1996: 43) put it, 'contains the means of its own correction'. While this view of consensus provides a basis of legitimacy for deliberative democracy, it does not tell us much about the outcome of deliberation. The first group of content-based solutions gives us a better idea of how deliberative democracy could be put into practice.

Such solutions also presuppose that it would indeed be possible to agree that deliberative forms of democracy produce the most legitimate outcomes. If we define deliberation in a more minimal sense, as group decision making through discussion, this may not be too problematic. However, if we add requirements for other-regardingness and other more controversial values, it may be that no such consensus over a deliberative model of democracy will emerge.

Deliberation could also serve to establish a consensus over using other decision-making methods. Thus a group could reach a deliberative consensus to use voting or strategic bargaining to resolve a problem. This highlights a very important point for the theory of deliberative democracy. While deliberative democrats do acknowledge the need to accommodate self-interest and to use non-deliberative decision-making mechanisms, these are all situated within a deliberative framework and their appropriateness needs to be determined through deliberative means. Thus in a model of deliberative democracy, deliberation is always the primary decision-making method, notwithstanding the use of voting or bargaining at times. This is a rather important point that is worth bearing in mind for evaluating the model of deliberative democracy.

Deliberation and Voting

Deliberation is perfectly compatible with the act of voting. First, even if decisions are made unanimously, at the very least a show of hands in necessary to ascertain that such unanimity exists. Second, political decisions need to be made in a timely manner. Voting offers a finite deadline to deliberators within which they have to come to a decision (Goodin 2008). Third, as we have seen above, under conditions of pluralism it is usually impossible to make a consensual decision without voting and compromise (Cohen 1989). What distinguishes deliberative theories of democracy is not an absence of voting, but the importance that is placed on the deliberation that goes beforehand and its legitimating power.

As we saw in Chapter 2, recent theories (Parkinson 2003, 2006; Saward 2003) advocate a more overarching theory of democracy that integrates deliberation with voting, protest, bargaining and other political action. Voting can take place in a micro deliberative forum; examples include a legislative chamber, a citizen jury, a general election to select representatives who take part in deliberative debate on behalf of the electorate, and referendums.

Most of the deliberative initiatives discussed in Chapter 7 combine elements of aggregative and deliberative democracy. The participatory budgeting (PB) procedure in Porto Alegre has a particularly significant aggregative component, as budget council members are elected and key neighbourhood priorities are selected through a majority rule procedure. Other procedures need to use aggregation simply to arrive at the final decision, as in the case of the British Columbia Citizens' Assembly (BCCA). Furthermore, the BCCA has also made use of a general referendum among the electorate that decided on whether to adopt the Assembly's recommendations (Warren and Pearse 2008).

Those citizens' juries and deliberative polls which have been run as quasi-experiments provide us with empirical information about the way in which deliberators change their views. They can provide crucial information about whether consensus or meta-agreement have increased, whether deliberators have become more informed, or whether there has been an increase in polarized preferences. However, as they do not directly contribute to political decision making, we need to be aware when interpreting results that real-world deliberation is likely to be even less close to the ideal than these experiments.

There is evidence that citizens are better informed on issues after deliberation than they were before. Farrar *et al.* (2010) find that after a deliberative poll the number of factual questions which deliberators could answer correctly increased from 36.8 per cent to 59.1 per cent. People also perceive themselves to be better informed after deliberation. After a deliberative poll in Hungary the proportion of those who considered themselves to be very well-informed or moderately well-informed about the situation of the Roma in Hungary increased from 74 per cent to 85 per cent (Magyar Agora, 2005). At the same time the proportion of factual questions answered correctly increased from 28 per cent to 42 per cent. Clearly, even after a day or two of deliberation people will still be unable to answer many of the questions correctly. But it is probably safe to say that after a longer period of deliberation, if deliberators took their duty seriously we would see a much more significant improvement.

There is also evidence that deliberation increases single-peakedness. This might point to an increase in agreement about the nature of the issue in deliberation, or in other words an increase in meta-consensus. An experiment using deliberative polling in New Haven found that single-peakedness increased for both of the topics discussed, albeit to a different extent (Fishkin *et al.* 2007; Farrar *et al.* 2010). Deliberation on the first issue, which was concerned with a possible extension of the local airport, only produced a marginal increase in single-peakedness. However, preferences were already well-structured at the start of deliberation, with the proportion of individuals whose preferences were single-peaked at 77 per cent, which eventually increased to 81 per cent. For the second issue, sharing tax revenues from new businesses between municipalities, the proportion of single-peaked preferences increased dramatically, from 52 per cent to 80 per cent. The authors explain this with the fact that in the months preceding deliberation airport extension was a much more prominent issue; therefore people had more developed preferences over it and were more aware of the underlying issue dimensions. Hence they had fewer opportunities to learn more about the issue dimensions involved and they were also less inclined to change their preferences. But as single-peakedness did increase for both issues, albeit to a different extent, the hypothesis that preferences will become more single-peaked during deliberation still holds based on this evidence.

Deliberation might induce a level of single-peakedness that virtually eliminates the presence of voting cycles. If this is the case, deliberation will succeed in its aim of reducing the instability and ambiguity that stems from voting. However, as the above example of the deliberative poll on airport extension shows, if an issue is salient in public discussions, in the media and in private conversation, preferences will already display a large degree of single-peakedness and thus meta-consensus is to a large extent already present. But as far as the need for some form of consensus in deliberation is concerned, we can say that while it is not feasible to assume that deliberation will result in a full consensus, an expectation of meta-consensus instead could be a viable alternative.

If meta-consensus is increased through deliberation, this means that we are relaxing the universal domain condition of Arrow's theorem. Under the universal domain condition, all logically possible preference orderings are admitted. But once preferences are single-peaked, this is no longer true. All logically possible preference orderings may still be permitted, but they would no longer always occur naturally. Deliberation might also restrict preferences through filtering out undesirable, such as racist preferences and maybe even by reducing the number of viable options to choose from. Thus deliberative democracy may offer us a way out of two of the problems identified by social choice theory: instability and impossibility.

The reason that it may be less useful against the problem of ambiguity is down to path dependence. Even in purely voting based systems of decision making, the sequence in which votes are taken over various issues can to a large extent determine the outcome, giving exceptional powers to the chair or agenda setter (Riker 1982). In the case of dialogue we are faced with a much more complex form of interaction. The order in which various arguments are introduced may be a powerful determinant of the final outcome. Thus, the problem of path dependence will persist even under deliberative democracy.

Publicity and Privacy

The circumstances under which deliberation is carried out can also contribute greatly to the quality of the final deliberative decision. In particular, whether deliberation is open or closed to the public appears to have a significant effect on the normative quality of deliberative decision making.

In the case of voting in mass electoral democracies, citizens are required to cast their votes secretly, in order to be free of bribery and intimidation. In legislatures, on the other hand, voting takes place in the open, allowing for greater accountability between legislators and their constituents. Deliberation faces some of the same demands of finding the balance between freedom of conscience and accountability.

The theory of deliberative democracy is centred around the notion of legitimacy. Thus, it seems clear that democratic deliberation ought to be public and deliberators ought to be accountable to their fellow citizens. However, there is also a demand for reasoned deliberation and an emphasis on individual preference and belief change as a result of such deliberation.

Juries deliberate in private, as a protection against undue influence from outside and to allow jurors the possibility of raising arguments without seeming to commit themselves to the defendant's guilt or innocence. Similarly, in political deliberation publicity and public commitment to policy positions might make it more difficult for political actors to then change their minds as a result of public deliberation, without seeming indecisive, and without losing their supporters. During open deliberation, individuals are also more likely to re-iterate their initial positions with varying forcefulness, rather than engaging in reasoned debate aimed at genuine persuasion and preference change. Thus at worst, deliberation can descend into demagoguery and what Chambers (2004) calls plebiscitary reason: public reasoning that appeals to preconceived notions, emotions and the lowest common denominator.

These arguments support the need to at least occasionally resort to secrecy in political deliberation. Within macro deliberation, meetings of like-minded individuals should be shielded from the public eye. In micro deliberation both citizens and politicians may fare better under conditions of privacy. This argument is supported by evidence. Steiner *et al.* (2004) have found that legislative chambers that use closed deliberation will use significantly more deliberative discourse.

However, secrecy is not without its dangers. If deliberators are shielded from public view, they may resort to arguments based on partial interests and bargaining instead. Thus, even if deliberation takes place privately, not only do its decisions need to be publicized, but also the reasoning that underlies those decisions. Furthermore, deciding when to deliberate in public and when to do so in private is tricky in itself. Gutmann and Thompson (1996) argue that secrecy is acceptable if it is compatible with the overall aims of deliberative democracy and if such secrecy can be approved through deliberative means. The ultimate test has to be whether secrecy or openness is more conducive to producing legitimate decisions.

Deliberation and Bargaining

Bargaining can be seen as a prime example of instrumental behaviour that thrives on and creates unequal power relationships. Thus, it seems inimical to the idea of a deliberative democracy. But, as we saw in Chapter 1, democracy can be conceptualized as a system that allows for multiple methods of decision making, depending on the context within which a decision is made (Saward 2003; Parkinson 2003, 2006).

If we allow deliberation to be accompanied by voting, the question arises whether we should relax the conditions of deliberation further and allow bargaining as well. While in the ideal model deliberation is assumed to be superior to bargaining, those authors who do mention it admit that it is a necessary part of politics. But little has been said so far about the kind of bargaining that is compatible with a deliberative model of democracy. Yet this is an important question, since deliberation is always situated among other political actions, such as voting, bargaining or protesting.

Habermas argues that decisions will be based on a 'complicated network of discourses and bargaining and not simply on moral discourses' (Habermas 1996a: 452), even in a primarily deliberative democracy. In *Between Facts and Norms* (1996) he adopts the point of view that bargaining can complement deliberation when the situation permits. Bargaining can be important because it gives greater priority to private interests, something which cannot be kept out of the political arena. Bargaining also becomes necessary, even in situations when deliberation would be optimal, if one side in the debate refuses to deliberate. Thus, bargaining can be a first-best or a second-best option, depending on the context.

According to Elster (1989), bargaining is an inefficient form of decision making. Among the factors that contribute to this inefficiency, he lists the cost of bargaining, the cost of trying to improve one's bargaining position, the danger of making excessive claims that cannot be met halfway, the tendency to disbelieve information that does not support one's position and the cost of establishing credibility (1989: 94). He also argues that both social norms and self-interest play a role in bargaining.

Integrating bargaining into the framework of a deliberative compromise could eliminate most of these inefficiencies. For example, deliberation could rule out informational biases – only listening to those who support our position. According to deliberative democrats, other-regardingness ought to check bargaining power. Equally, allowing bargaining to form part of the democratic decision-making procedure cannot mean that we accommodate those who are completely unwilling to engage in reasonable deliberation or to accept compromise. Following the conditions that Habermas (1996a) specifies, we can define bargaining under a deliberative framework as a decision-making mechanism with outcomes which are acceptable to everyone and which are better than no agreement at all, and which furthermore excludes those who withdraw from deliberation completely and prohibits the exploitation of one part of the group by the other.

An important reason for supporting bargaining under a deliberative framework is that while we can find a moral dimension in most political issues, it may be possible to decide some of them primarily on grounds of self-interest. Gutmann and Thompson (1996) give trade negotiations as an example. But even in these cases the moral merits of the outcome have to be properly considered and bargaining should be guided by the principle of reciprocity (Gutmann and Thompson 1996: 72). While trade negotiations might have an obvious moral aspect, there is a range of options which are morally acceptable, but which nevertheless benefit the two parties to different degrees. These morally acceptable options could be identified through deliberation. Thus once we make sure that a trade agreement is not exploitative and does not jeopardize human rights, we cannot object to reaching a decision through bargaining.

The problem with this distinction is that it requires us to draw a line between primarily moral and all other disagreements. Gutmann and Thompson argue that disputes over redistribution and welfare should be resolved by deliberation, while trade agreements such as the North American Free Trade Agreement (NAFTA) can be negotiated through bargaining. But trade agreements could easily be reframed in terms of moral arguments. Barriers to free trade affect the life chances of those in poorer countries significantly. Therefore trade negotiations can be said to have a significant moral component. Of course, trade negotiations have the added complication that they are conducted between countries. But similar examples can be found in domestic politics as well, such as negotiations between employers and trade unions in corporatist countries. In these cases theorists need to invoke democratic deliberation as the framework within which it can be decided whether an issue can be legitimately resolved through bargaining.

All the above arguments see bargaining as subordinate to the supposedly morally superior, other-regarding deliberative procedure. This is not a realistic assumption. In the cases where bargaining took place, it would exist alongside deliberation, rather than being subsumed under its more demanding standards of behaviour and attitudes.

Democracy consists of a number of decision-making mechanisms, each with its own strengths and weaknesses: deliberation, voting, bargaining, protest and so on. There will be situations when deliberation is the most appropriate decision-making procedure, but there will also be situations when we need to use other mechanisms. We need to understand and evaluate each of these on its own terms. It does not make sense to evaluate the legitimacy of a bargaining process based on the standards set for democratic deliberation.

Some would question whether it is bargaining at all if all agreed on a common goal, even if it were as vague as agreeing on a policy for health provision, but could not agree on the way in which this goal could be reached. Bargaining is usually seen as a mechanism for dividing goods, rather than choosing between decisions that will give everyone equal pay-offs. It is clear that one can bargain over different ways to divide $100. It is not so clear that one can bargain over whether healthcare should be provided privately or publicly. Brennan and Goodin (2001) and Goodin (2003) argue that the latter scenario can still be called bargaining as each individual has different views on the pay-offs which the community receives from different decisions. One person might believe that we would all be better off if healthcare was provided privately and another person might believe that we would all be better off if it was provided publicly. In this case there is room for bargaining over our beliefs, as we both have different expectations about the pay-offs that the two different policies would generate. Thus, for each participant the expected pay-off of choosing his preferred policy will be different from the expected pay-off of choosing any other policy.

Deliberative democracies will no doubt have to deal with situations where goods can be bargained over and divided in the same way as we can divide $100. Welfare policies are an obvious example of this, but the example of trade negotiations above also falls into this category. There will also be instances where different individuals or groups favour different ways of proceeding to reach a certain goal. In these cases bargaining in the sense that Brennan and Goodin use the term will be possible.

However, there will be cases where the choices available are so different that it is not possible to bargain over them. Abortion is a classic example. There is a binary choice between either allowing abortion or not. There is only a possibility of bargaining once one allows for the possibility of abortion, where there is space to argue for anything between making abortion legal for the first few weeks only and allowing it up to the end of pregnancy. But when two options are completely divergent bargaining is not possible. Another example is whether we should allow pictures of Mohammed to be published or not. It is unlikely that those who argue against it will settle for depicting the prophet partially or in a positive light. There will be cases where there will be disagreement over the nature of goal we should reach – in these cases bargaining may not help us even in a deliberative setting.

Not all theorists agree that bargaining is a necessary element of deliberative politics. Bohman (1996) argues that bargaining reduces deliberative democracy to a *modus vivendi.* Furthermore, bargaining asks the impossible in the case of deep conflicts, when it treats deeply held beliefs as something negotiable. As he does not agree with the viability of Rawls's overlapping consensus, he does not share Rawls's optimism that over time such a *modus vivendi* can become something that will satisfy his democratic requirements more closely.

Out of necessity, bargaining has to remain a part of politics even in a deliberative democracy. But just like voting, it will introduce further complications for the theory of deliberative democracy. Since they cannot always be subsumed under the deliberative framework, deliberation has to co-exist with other decision-making processes which do not follow the standards set down by deliberative theorists.

Conclusion

Like all theories of how we can make collective political choices, the theory of deliberative democracy needs to present a clear argument as to how it will lead to actual decisions made in a timely manner. Once we acknowledge that in plural societies consensus will be the exception, rather than the norm, we can integrate deliberation with other forms of decision making, such as voting or bargaining.

Thus deliberation will be part of a complex system of democratic decision-making mechanisms, each appropriate under different circumstances and each conforming to different ideal, democratic standards. A theory of democracy that focuses solely on deliberation is in danger of undervaluing other ways of making decisions, such as voting. This is not to say that deliberation is not a valuable and indispensable part of democratic process and that there is no need to foster more democratic deliberation.

The last three chapters have evaluated some of the theoretical aspects of deliberative democracy in great detail. The next two chapters will examine a range of ways in which deliberative democracy can be implemented in practice, both through new, citizen-focused initiatives and in existing institutions.

6

Implementing Deliberation

The theory of deliberative democracy has clear practical applications and democratic theorists have actively promoted it as a way of reforming contemporary democratic practice. This chapter and the next will examine how the theories presented so far can be and have been implemented.

Democracy is by no means a static system. There have already been major changes to liberal democracies in the past, such as the extension of the franchise or the introduction of secret ballots. Yet liberal democracy does not flourish equally in all countries. There is a large literature in political science examining the preconditions for democracy and the causes of democratization. One of the first notable examples is de Tocqueville's *Democracy in America* (1945). New waves of democratization during the twentieth century served both to increase the data available to scholars and to fuel interest in what conditions are needed for the development of stable democracies. Arguments highlight the importance of political culture (Almond and Verba 1963/1989), economic development (Lipset 1959), the role of elites (Rustow 1970) and the role of class structure (Rueschmayer *et al.* 1992).

Equally, it is likely that deliberative democracy would not flourish in all places and at all times. The question is whether it would be possible to introduce deliberative reform in existing democratic countries.

Macro Deliberation in Practice

It appears undeniable that macro deliberation – deliberation in the wider public sphere – does take place in contemporary liberal democracies. The existence of public debate, a free press and civil society

121

groups all contribute to its existence. Yet it is difficult to assess macro deliberation in practice. There are no clear ways of measuring how much deliberation takes place in the public sphere, what its quality is and how many people participate directly. Part of the reason is that macro deliberation can take place across so many venues and over such a long period of time.

Probably the most realistic assessment is that existing democracies are already deliberative to some extent, but do not fully comply with the standards set out by non-ideal theories of deliberative democracy. Thus deliberation needs to be extended so that a larger proportion of political decisions are decided through it and more citizens and officials participate in deliberation. A parallel can be drawn with franchise; just because some already had the vote in nineteenth-century England, this did not mean that the franchise could not be widened by being extended to all social classes and to women.

A big problem with observing macro deliberation is that there is disagreement even about the limits of what counts as deliberation. Should private conversations be included, for example? Personal conversations about politics are often not civil towards those not present, neither, frequently, are they reasoned. Gutmann and Thompson (1999) exclude them from their model of deliberation precisely because they do not conform to the values of reciprocity, publicity and accountability that democratic deliberation is expected to fulfill. Thus, they argue that such talk should take place without being held to the high standards of the theory. However, this reasoning excludes most democratic political talk from the macro deliberative model, making its definition too narrow.

The same problem applies when it comes to fostering macro deliberation. If we have no clear idea where and how it takes place and who participates, we are most likely not going to know what kinds of policies would be most effective in increasing the level of public deliberation and whether existing policies are achieving their intended outcomes.

The difficulty of designing, let alone funding, a large-scale study of macro deliberation means that no such studies exist yet. We may be able to make inferences from studies of political participation, but these have not focused specifically on the deliberative aspect of participation. While we can use proxies, such as the number of citizens who have actively contributed to political campaigns, attended certain public meetings or contacted their representatives, this would only capture participation in a small part of the public sphere.

Instead, there are detailed studies which examine various forms of political participation in societies, as well as citizen attitudes and social capital. The books by Gamson (1992) and Cramer Walsh (2004) are two excellent examples of recent work that seeks to analyze the characteristics of political talk among citizens. Verba *et al.* (1995) carried out an impressively large-scale survey study of political participation in the US. The think tank Demos has put together an index of 'everyday democracy', ranking EU countries (Skidmore and Bound 2008). But these studies still cannot tell us how deliberative a democracy is. At most they give us snapshots of various aspects of civic life in various countries.

As I mentioned when I defined it in Chapter 1, macro deliberation is often a by-product of other social activities (Cramer Walsh 2004). This raises the importance of this kind of activity and what is normally termed social capital. In the following section I will offer a brief overview of some of the concepts which could be most influential for the success of macro deliberation: trust, social capital and political culture.

Trust, social capital and political culture

The way different individuals relate to each other is captured by the concepts of trust and social capital. Moreover, individuals relate not only to each other, but also to political institutions; this is political culture.

Trust is a commonly used concept which describes the extent to which we feel that we can rely on other individuals. Generalized trust relates to trusting others in society in general. This is the kind of trust measured by survey questions asking people whether they perceive other people as trustworthy. By contrast, interpersonal trust is trust placed in specific individuals. Interpersonal trust is important in politics, as decision making is a process that takes place between individuals (Leach and Sabatier 2005). For the purposes of deliberative democracy, generalized trust might make it easier to initiate deliberative discussions, but it is going to be interpersonal trust that will allow deliberators to work together constructively.

Social capital is concerned with the networks and relationships between individuals in society. A society with rich individual networks based on goodwill, trust and reciprocity has high levels of social capital. Social capital is reflected in and can be measured through a number of different variables. These include religious attendance, the number of friends an average person has, volunteering, philanthropy, civic participation and participation in different groups such as bridge clubs.

Deliberation is an inter-personal affair and it can both draw on and build up social capital. It draws on social capital when it requires participants to extend existing ties between each other to the political forum. Putnam (2000) links social capital both to generalized reciprocity and generalized trust – that is, willingness to act kindly towards and to trust others, whether we have known them in the past or not. These are both factors that can contribute towards successful deliberation. It can also be argued that social capital develops a greater sense of community and, through this, civic duty. At the same time deliberation can also work to build social capital. Interactions between individuals develop new networks, which enable the group to develop arguments and decisions together. Deliberative groups would ideally have to build and draw on bridging social capital that connects individuals in different social and economic groups. That is, individuals who hold different points of view and lead different kinds of lives would need to get together in order to make decisions together.

The problem with the social capital approach is that it is broad and often intangible. Measuring it can be difficult, as group participation or volunteering will inevitably be proxies for a less tangible concept. There are two main reasons why social capital may not be as important as often portrayed.

First, and most important, there is no clear evidence that social capital has a significant effect on participation in politics (Jackman and Miller 1998; Scheufele and Shah 2000). Putnam argues that higher levels of social capital will result in higher levels of political participation. But this requires a logical leap. Just because an individual enjoys playing bridge at a bridge club, salsa dancing with a local group, has many friends or attends church regularly, this does not imply that he will also enjoy or feel a duty to participate or get involved in politics. Thus high levels of social capital will not affect the likelihood of individuals becoming willing participants in deliberative groups.

Second, many of these groups are homogeneous, that is, they bring together individuals who share common interests and are likely to view the world in a similar way. They are characterized by bonding social capital: relationships between individuals in similar positions. This is different from deliberative settings, where group members would come from heterogeneous backgrounds and could hold very different views from each other. Thus the pre-existence of high levels of social capital, measured in the form of group membership, will not necessarily lead to better deliberation, as most social capital will be of the bonding rather than the bridging form.

Advanced industrial and post-industrial societies do display fairly high levels of social capital and trust and they are often described as important variables when it comes to the stability of representative democratic regimes. In fact, societies would be unlikely to survive without them. Very few people do not belong to groups, or have no ties to friends and family, although these ties are not always strong (according to the General Household Survey: see Walker *et al.* 2001), 20 per cent of the UK population feel they have neither a satisfactory friendship nor relatives network). In general, society also requires a level of trust to function. We need to place some basic trust in others in order to get on with daily life. These levels of trust and social capital are sufficient to allow individuals to start participating in deliberative groups. Repeated interactions will of course build further social capital and trust, but their lack will not hamper the introduction of deliberative democracy.

Another strand of research identifies democratic political culture as one of the main preconditions for democracy. Almond and Verba (1963/1989: 13), in their study of five countries, define it as 'the particular distribution of patterns of orientation towards political objects among the members of a nation'. Thus political culture determines how most individuals within a society relate to the political system. This encompasses how they think about, feel about and evaluate political processes. According to Almond and Verba, democracy is best supported by a participant political culture, where citizens expect to be members of a political community who can influence policies. By contrast, parochial political cultures, where there are no specialized political actors, support traditional, such as feudal, systems and subject cultures in which citizens submit themselves to specialist political elites, best support authoritarian regimes.

The existence of a participant political culture is clearly crucial for deliberative democracy, but it is not sufficient. Almond and Verba find that while citizens in stable democracies are unlikely to participate in politics, they perceive that they would be able to participate, should they need or wish to do so. In order for democracies to become more deliberative, citizens would not only need to believe that it is possible for them to participate, they would also need to be more willing than they are at the moment to seize those opportunities. Furthermore, deliberative democracy is more likely to flourish in political cultures where there are no taboo subjects, such as the subject of the monarchy in Thailand.

Trust, social capital and political culture are each important variables for the development of deliberative democracy. Citizens of liberal representative democracies already display levels of trust and social capital that are sufficient for some form of deliberation to exist. But in order for deliberative democracy to flourish our political culture would have to change. This is of course perfectly in line with the aims of the deliberative project. Rather than just being aware that it is possible for us to participate, should we wish to do so, we would need to be more proactive about getting involved in politics and deliberative debates. This may prove to be problematic given the problems of motivation most citizens will face.

Deliberative Reform

If we are serious about making democracies more deliberative or about introducing new deliberative initiatives, we need to consider what would be necessary for this. I will first consider whether individuals would be capable of engaging in deeper and more frequent deliberation, and motivated to do so. Then I will examine how easily the existing political system allows for deliberative reform.

Given the prominence of the theory of deliberative democracy, it is somewhat surprising that democratic deliberation is often seen in isolation, with the background conditions and outcomes of the process only making rare and fleeting appearances. And when these conditions and outcomes do make an appearance, it is only with reference to fulfilling the normative requirements of the theory. The conditions that would allow deliberation to take place in the first place, such as a citizenry with sufficient time and interest to participate in deliberation, are often neglected. The following will address part of this shortcoming.

Abilities and attitudes

Successful participation in deliberative decision-making processes requires individuals to possess certain cognitive abilities and psychological attitudes. These relate to the cognitive demands of deliberation at all stages of the debate, from understanding arguments to making well-reasoned decisions. They enable individuals to act in a manner which theorists say is normatively desirable, in particular to be open to new arguments and to be other-regarding (for example, Elster 1986; Gutmann and Thompson 1996. 2004).

Deliberation demands that individuals perform a multitude of cognitively complex tasks (Reykowski 2006). They need to be able to concentrate on potentially complicated arguments put forward during long discussions. They need to be able to interpret new facts and arguments correctly and evaluate them critically. Furthermore, they need to be able themselves to form logical arguments, which must be justified to others, and communicate these effectively. Different people have differing abilities to perform these tasks.

Moreover, we may overestimate our ability to reach better decisions through deliberation by relying on a false folk theory of learning (Lupia 2002). We know if we correct our beliefs after learning relevant new facts, but we are not usually aware of the many cases when we fail to correct an incorrect belief because we have never encountered any information that forces us to do so, or when we simply ignore that information. Thus when we informally 'test' the theory, perceived successes will far outnumber failures.

Ordinary citizens apportion relatively little time and effort to these cognitively demanding processes, as work, family, relationships and daily life already take up much of their resources. However, it should be within the reach of nearly all citizens to arrive at an adequately reasoned argument on specific, not overly technical issues after a period of deliberation. This is what the jury system in Anglo-Saxon countries relies on. The beliefs might still be incorrect ones (Pincione and Tesón 2006), but as individuals have spent more effort on acquiring and processing information, they are likely to be better than they would have been if no deliberation had taken place. Thus while cognitive demands do affect the quality of deliberation we can expect from ordinary citizens and the resulting outcomes, they do not affect the possibility that they would be able to participate in some form of deliberative process.

Apart from cognitive capacities, normative theories of deliberation also require citizens to hold certain attitudes, such as openness to new ideas and experiences (McCrae and Costa 2003) and other-regardingness (Elster 1986; Mansbridge 1990). These attitudes are also some of the likely results of deliberative discussions, as citizens learn to 'launder' their preferences (Goodin 1986) and increasingly come to respect and tolerate the views of others (Mutz 2006). However, a minimal level of tolerance and openness is necessary in order to make citizens willing to start deliberating. Deliberative democracy would require a higher degree of political tolerance and support for civil liberties and democracy than liberal representative forms of democracy, as citizens would need to engage with views different from their own more directly. Studies have shown that the internalization of democratic values leads to greater tolerance (Sullivan and Transue 1999); therefore citizens of democratic countries would be better prepared for deliberation than citizens of non-democratic regimes. Perceptions of threat reduce the extent to which individuals are tolerant; therefore it is important to ensure that all deliberators feel that the process is impartial and takes their views into account.

Citizens of democratic countries already possess sufficient levels of tolerance and openness to have some kind of deliberative debate, even if this would not always approximate the ideal. The clearest evidence for this is that deliberative polls, meetings and experiments do not simply break down, but exhibit some measure of success (Fishkin *et al.* 2002; Gastil and Levine 2005; Warren and Pearse 2008; and many more). Thus it seems that neither cognitive capacities nor attitudes provide problems for deliberative democracy, as long as we accept that they will not be present to an extent sufficient to produce ideal deliberation.

Motivation

However, individuals do not only need the ability to deliberate. They also need to have the will to do so. Deliberation requires citizens to acquire new information and to update their beliefs based on it. It also requires them to hold well-reasoned positions, rather than instinctive opinions. Yet it has long been a widely shared view in political science, especially among rational choice theorists, that individuals have little incentive to learn about politics (Downs 1957; Aldrich

1993; Popkin 1993; Mueller 2003). Turnout at elections has been falling for decades, political apathy is viewed as a common problem for all developed democracies and most voters appear to be shockingly uninformed in surveys (Delli Carpini and Keeter 1996). Downs (1957) was one of the first to describe this rational ignorance on the part of voters. Seeking out new information is costly and only brings limited benefits to citizens. Reading newspapers and watching the news on television is time-consuming, not to mention for some people also very boring. Therefore only those who enjoy the fact of keeping up to date or those who can expect higher benefits by using their knowledge to influence others will engage in such a costly activity.

Most citizens, however, will rely on shortcuts and heuristics to form judgements about politics. Information acquired during day-to-day life serves as an important source of knowledge about economic and current affairs (Grofman and Withers 1993; Popkin 1993) and party labels offer an easy indication as to candidates' positions. Average citizens also rely on lobby groups, community leaders and whistle blowers to let them know if things are not going well and their interests are not being represented in politics, rather than following politics closely themselves (Popkin 1993).

The above picture, of course, applies to an aggregative political system where most citizens' engagement with politics is limited to turning up at the polling station every few years. This is a situation that deliberative democrats would like to remedy. So would the calculus of rational ignorance be different for deliberative citizens?

It is sometimes assumed that participating in deliberation will make citizens more engaged with politics (Gutmann and Thompson 1996). They will become better informed, as deliberation helps participants learn new facts (Manin 1987). Deliberative programmes could also help those who have never previously had the opportunity to become engaged in politics to get involved. It is easy to see that this could especially benefit poorer and more disadvantaged segments of society. Participatory budget projects in the Brazilian cities of Porto Alegre (Baiocchi 2003) and Belo Horizonte (Souza 2001) provided an opportunity for people from poorer areas with little education to participate in deliberative forums and become representatives for their neighbourhoods. Residents in Porto Alegre reported how they learnt to participate from those more experienced or better educated than themselves, even though at the beginning they did not know what they were expected to do (Baiocchi 2003: 53).

This view, however, makes two key assumptions. The first is that people *want to* participate in deliberation, either because they enjoy the act itself or because of the benefits they receive from this mode of decision making. The second is that people *should* participate in politics, as this is a civic virtue which all citizens should engage in. The following argument will take on the first of these assumptions:that people are motivated to participate in political deliberation.

Participating in political deliberation is a form of collective action that is aimed at securing outcomes that everyone will benefit from, regardless of whether or not they participated themselves. These outcomes can be concrete policies or they can be intangible benefits like an increase in civic virtue, tolerance and respect for others.

The collective action problem (Olson 1965; Ostrom 1990; Tuck 2008) tells us that the individual cost of participating in activities aimed at securing a collective good will outweigh the benefits received by each individual when it is taken into account that individuals will receive those benefits, no matter whether they participated or not. This leads to free-riding behaviour, as most people will rely on others to get the work done. In order for deliberation to be successful, the collective action problem needs to be overcome. This is by no means impossible. One of the most potent examples of it is the paradox of turnout. The cost of voting is relatively high compared to the benefits each individual voter will receive from having his or her preferred party elected. Yet millions of people still turn out to vote on election day. Thus it appears that a simple cost–benefit analysis does not give us a full account of what motivates individuals to vote (Dowding 2005) and other explanatory variables need to be added to the benefit side of the equation, such as habit, a sense of duty or the sense of enjoyment that participation provides, despite the fact that these are difficult to quantify. The practice of deliberative democracy would need to face a similar cost–benefit analysis. Given that the cost of deliberation is generally high, and certainly much higher than the cost of casting a vote, are the benefits sufficient to compensate for this?

In general, two aspects of deliberation can make or break people's interest in participating. The first is how interested people are in the topic of the debate. The second is whether they perceive that their participation has made a genuine difference.

Let us first look at the question of personal interest. People are more interested in issues which affect them directly or issues on which they hold strong views. These two will often coincide. Thus local, neighbourhood issues and high-profile national issues will generate more interest. The cost of deliberating over these issues will be relatively low, as participants will already be to some extent informed about the facts and arguments and this is complemented by relatively high personal benefits from participating. However, people are also likely to have strong pre-formed judgements about these issues, and therefore belief change is less likely to occur (Bartels 1993; Farrar *et al.* 2010), thus making deliberation less socially and politically useful and conforming less to the normative theory of deliberation.

Citizens will be less well-informed about obscure, complicated issues. While they might change their opinion about these more easily, deliberators will need more time to learn the necessary facts and arguments to come to a reasoned decision. This raises the cost of deliberation in these cases significantly, while the personal benefits are lower, as these issues will be of less interest to deliberators and the outcomes may affect them less personally. Thus deliberation would here be more socially useful, while at the same time it is personally more costly and less beneficial. This could lead to the perverse outcome that citizens will be less motivated to participate in deliberation in cases that are more socially beneficial. We can assume that other non-quantifiable benefits, such as a sense of fulfilling one's civic duty, would be equal in both of these cases.

The second aspect of deliberation that affects the benefits each deliberator receives is the material difference that their participation makes. One of the reasons why the benefits of voting are so low is that the benefit of each vote must be multiplied by the probability that it will be pivotal, that is, that it will actually make a difference to the outcome. This number is infinitesimally small in a large electorate. Deliberation faces the same problem from two perspectives: first, the participation of each individual will actually have to matter and, second, the results of deliberation have to be translated into public policy.

The impact of individuals' participation is much harder to assess than in the case of voting. Each vote counts equally, but as we saw in Chapter 4, not every argument is equal in a deliberative discussion. Thus those who feel that their voice will have little impact will be less motivated to participate. And these are likely to be those who are already disadvantaged in society. Due to the complexity of the calculation, it may even appear to citizens that the cost of participation is even higher and the benefits even lower than in reality, thus compounding the collective action problem.

Whether the outcomes of deliberation will make an actual impact depends on the political will to make it happen. I will discuss this in more detail in the next section. For the time being, suffice it to say that if participants in deliberative groups feel that their decisions and their deliberations have little impact on actual policy, they are unlikely to feel motivated to keep turning up. Material benefits would need to appear in a timely fashion in order to convince citizens that the process was working. If very little changes in individuals' day-to-day lives as a result of deliberation, then the material benefits of participating may not be enough to lure people along, unless they get other significant benefits from the process, such as personal enjoyment or a sense of fulfilling their responsibility.

In the cases where these benefits cannot be met, the individual cost of participating in deliberation is high. One of the greatest constraints is of course time. Time constraints can limit the range of people who participate in meetings on a regular basis. Poorer people working in multiple jobs, professionals working long hours and those with small children in general have less time and energy to participate in meetings held in the evenings and at weekends. At the other end of the scale the self-employed, stay-at-home wives and husbands, pensioners, students, those with flexible schedules, part-time workers and the unemployed have more time to participate (Souza 2001). There is evidence from the Porto Alegre project that women are less likely to participate, as holding a full-time job and carrying out household duties leaves them with little spare time (Baiocchi 2003). In the Brazilian participatory budget projects some of the poorest sections of the population lack motivation to participate in the process as their primary concern is day-to-day personal survival, rather than the infrastructure and public goods projects that the budget focuses on (Souza 2001).

The costs for each individual citizen of participating in either micro or macro deliberation will often outweigh the benefits. In the absence of other significant personal factors, such as individual interest in politics or a sense of civic duty, most citizens are unlikely to be motivated to participate in deliberation.

Those most likely to be active in deliberative forums are those who are active in politics now. It is important to note that even in successful cases, such as the deliberative forums in Porto Alegre, the deliberators were self-selected. Many people dislike participating in public meetings or even discussing politics informally. Most people prefer to avoid confrontation when it comes to political disagreement and prefer to discuss politics with like-minded people (Mutz 2006). Furthermore, many feel shy or feel they cannot argue their case as persuasively as others do (Mansbridge 1980). These people are less likely to participate in formal deliberation. And self-selection can have dangerous consequences, as the unrepresented may lose out in the process. Fung (2004: 105–6) argues that self-selection and relatively low participation rates are not a problem, as citizens may have to choose between a number of forums to participate in and only get involved in one or two which they are most motivated to attend. But the problem is that if individuals can choose between a large number of groups, their efforts will be fragmented and each forum may be captured by a homogeneous special interest group.

Overall, individual motivation may significantly limit the extent to which citizens are willing to participate in deliberative projects. This should not pose a problem as long as we admit that deliberative discussions would not extend to cover all citizens. There are already a large number of individuals who are sufficiently interested in politics to play a part in the political process, whether as elected representatives at the national or local level or as civil society activists. There will always be people who are motivated enough and capable enough to successfully participate in deliberative processes. Additional incentives, such as a cash reward for participating, could further increase their number. If deliberative democracy is defined in this way, rather than as a debate that encompasses the whole of society, then its individual-level preconditions will be met. However, in this case more attention needs to be paid to mechanisms that make deliberation representative and accountable.

Political will

Individual motivation emerges as a significant factor when it comes to increasing the quantity and quality of democratic deliberation. The next question is whether this problem of motivation is also present when it comes to reforming political institutions. How easily would existing political elites warm to deliberative democracy? Here

I am concerned with the best way of introducing more deliberation into the political arena and I will discuss specific deliberative initiatives in greater detail in the next chapter.

In much of the literature, deliberative democracy is assumed to supersede current aggregative arrangements, or in other words liberal representative democracies. Dahl characterizes liberal representative democracies as polyarchies (Dahl 1989). He identifies seven distinctive characteristics of such political systems: (1) government decisions are made by officials elected in (2) free and fair elections under (3) universal suffrage; citizens have (4) a right to run for office, (5) a right to freedom of expression, (6) a right to access alternative sources of information and (7) a right to associational autonomy (Dahl 1989: 221).

Of course not all countries have such systems already in place. Some countries are not yet democratic and many others have only become democracies relatively recently and are not yet consolidated democracies. Illiberal (Zakaria 1997) and delegative (O'Donnell 1994) democracies are examples of nominally democratic regimes that lack many of the features of consolidated liberal democracies. It is unlikely that these systems will be able to introduce deliberative democracy straight away, without developing a stable democratic regime first, as many of the preconditions I looked at in the previous sections of the chapter, such as deeply rooted democratic values and a democratic political culture, will be missing (for an opposing argument, see O'Flynn 2006 and Dryzek 2006).

In democratic regimes the rules of the democratic decision-making process are enshrined in written or unwritten constitutions. These determine the way in which elections are carried out and policies are made. These constitutional rules provide legitimacy and stability for democratic laws and policies and are normally much more difficult to change than other laws, requiring a supermajority or even repeated supermajorities in the legislature. Thus at the institutional level the rules of the game need to offer opportunities for deliberative reform to be introduced.

For many, deliberative reforms take the form of introducing new, deliberative political institutions alongside existing ones. These reforms assume substantial institutional change, whether that involves nationwide deliberative polls (Ackermann and Fishkin 2004) or compulsory deliberative jury duty (Leib 2004). It is usually difficult to introduce institutional changes which are this substantial. In many countries they require constitutional reform, which needs to be approved by a 'supermajority'. The question is whether politicians would have incentives to introduce such wide-ranging deliberative reforms.

In their detailed analysis of what deliberation day might look like, Ackermann and Fishkin (2004) describe the increased pressures US presidential candidates would face during their campaigns if the new institutions were introduced. Not only would citizens discuss the issues and candidates during the course of a special nationwide deliberation day held before each election, but the most common questions would also be addressed by candidates in a televised debate. Presidential candidates would be evaluated based on different criteria from those that are used now once they had to face deliberation day. This would increase uncertainty about the outcome of elections and the established campaign machine would need to be significantly modified to deal with these changed circumstances. And it would not even be guaranteed that citizens would be interested in this new institution and would keep turning up every four years.

Deliberation day would change the electoral system by making voters more informed about candidates and by possibly changing the views held on various issues by the median voter, who is considered to be decisive in an election, thereby increasing candidates' uncertainty about the policies that would be attractive to the electorate. Other arrangements, such as deliberative assemblies, would add new veto players to the political landscape or could change the agenda-setting and gate-keeping powers of political actors.

Given these pressures, incumbents may not be very amenable to introducing new deliberative institutions. They have a vested interest in preserving the status quo, since this is what brought them into power and allows them to stay in power. Even in the case of lame duck politicians, their close ties to their party and political allies who still face further elections stay their hands when they consider dabbling in deliberative experiments. We must remember that deliberative institutions along the lines of deliberation day are not minor changes and could alter the status quo drastically. Deliberation is only one option available to politicians for resolving conflict.

Politicians are of course not purely office-seeking. They also have process-oriented concerns (Bowler *et al.* 2006), that is, they care about the fairness and adequacy of the system that can bring them into power. In general, elites are more partial towards democratic values

(Sullivan and Transue 1999) than the general population. Thus they may find the idea of increased deliberation attractive in itself. But concern for the quality of democratic processes is only rewarded by the electorate to a limited extent. Thus on the supply side of democratic innovations politicians will have little motivation to introduce deliberative institutions.

Furthermore, there is also a lack of popular demand for these institutions. There is no immediately obvious urgent need to make democracy more deliberative. The introduction of secret ballots was a reaction to the threat of voter intimidation and bribery, acts that both politicians and citizens were rightfully concerned about, as they distorted elections unacceptably. What threat to democratic ideas does deliberative democracy respond to? Deliberation might respond to the widespread feeling that there is a democratic deficit due to voter apathy and distrust of politicians (Hibbing and Theiss-Morse 2002). These are certainly themes which are taken up regularly by politicians, civil society groups and the media. But the idea of increased deliberation between citizens does not appear to have caught on outside the academic sphere, despite relatively widely publicized deliberative experiments. While general apathy and disenchantment with politics is frequently cited, more deliberative arrangements are not mentioned as a possible solution.

One could argue that the reason for this is the relative novelty of the deliberative project. But participatory democracy, which has been popular in academia for a much longer time, has failed to catch on as well. The lack of enthusiasm reveals a lack of motivation and incentives on the part of citizens to embrace costly, time- and resource-consuming deliberative reforms. Deliberative democracy fails where participatory democracy has failed – there is a sense of disbelief that it will work, that corrupt politicians and busy citizens can make it work (Hibbing and Theiss-Morse 2002). Thus deliberative democracy is not well-known and popular enough and the need for it is not strong enough to entice politicians to support large-scale reforms. But smaller, more incremental improvements may be more likely to succeed.

If deliberation is not to be introduced from above, another possibility is to introduce it from below – through local government and civil society initiatives. Reforms could take the form of establishing small-scale formal deliberative groups or encouraging public sphere deliberation among the wider electorate. This would circumvent the lack of political will at the national level and may motivate ordinary citizens to participate more directly.

Most documented deliberative or quasi-deliberative projects are grass-roots initiatives of this type. Fung (2004) gives the example of initiatives in the Chicago police and state school systems which give residents and parents greater input into how those services are run. Fung's study finds that this kind of citizen involvement had a significant positive impact. Other such initiatives include the participatory budget project in Brazil, first introduced in Porto Alegre after the left-wing PT party won the city's municipal elections. The process allows residents to set their own priorities for the city's annual budget through a series of meetings. The general population only participates in the first meeting, where participants for further, ongoing deliberative groups are selected. The scheme was adopted by other cities as well, with varying success. But these projects are affected by the problem of individual motivation to participate in politics.

Moreover, even if citizens have the will to get together and deliberate, their decisions still need to be implemented rather than ignored. Cohen and Rogers (2003) point out that the success of such projects is often ensured because there is a political will to carry out the kinds of policies favoured by the deliberative groups, and this will would have existed even without any kind of deliberative procedure. Thus these projects were successful because their decisions coincided with those preferred by individuals, groups and institutions that were part of the existing power structure. This can be seen in Porto Alegre where the results of the participatory budget coincided with the PT party's aims, such as increasing taxes.

Cohen and Rogers argue that another indicator of success is that these projects focus on a relatively small and well-defined area of public policy. Citizens are not required to set their own agenda and have to decide within budgetary constraints which are imposed on them from outside. They also need to learn about a relatively limited area of policy making. This simplifies their task considerably and does not pose excessive cognitive demands.

The current state of empirical research into deliberation does not yet tell us what distinguishes successful deliberative enterprises from unsuccessful ones. The reason for this is that only successful cases are studied in detail. It would be interesting to see more studies of deliberative projects that have *failed* in order to identify which independent variables cause success or failure.

A second possibility is to strengthen the deliberative elements of existing institutions. Legislatures are already deliberative institutions, although the kind of deliberation present there is often very different from the kind of deliberation advocated by political theorists. Legislatures are by their very nature adversarial arenas, where divisions about most issues exist along party lines. Steiner *et al.* (2003, 2004) developed a discourse quality index which is a quantitative measure of how far political discourse in legislatures approximates deliberative ideals. The index measures whether legislators were able to state their arguments without interruptions, the level and content of justifications offered, the respect legislators showed towards other groups and other arguments and the extent to which political discourse aimed at building a consensus. When they applied this index to legislative debates in Switzerland, Germany, the UK and the US (Steiner *et al.* 2004), they found the greatest differences with regard to the level of respect legislators displayed towards others. Furthermore their study found that the quality of discourse is higher in consociational and presidential systems, where the number of veto players is large, in second chambers, when the debates were not public and when issues under discussion are not polarized. The difference between different kinds of systems was in any case relatively small, and many of the institutional variables that Steiner *et al.* found to make a difference would face opposition for the same reasons that more sweeping deliberative reforms would.

Executives could become more deliberative in two broad ways. Firstly, deliberation within the executive could be encouraged. This, however, is problematic as executive decision-making processes lack exposure to the public eye, and it would only involve a small group of career politicians. Secondly, the executive could commission groups of citizens to conduct debates on its behalf, along the lines of citizens' juries. Governing parties already make extensive use of focus groups. However, if the decisions citizens' juries reach are regularly at odds with the government's own policy positions, this can endanger this project. Unfortunately deliberative ideas, such as the UK government inviting people to comment on government policy through an online forum on the Downing Street website, are often symbolic gestures that have no effect on actual policy making (Wright 2006).

Public services could organize stakeholder meetings in order to allow their clients to have more input into how they are run. This is especially useful for public services which are active locally, such as healthcare providers, schools or the police. Nevertheless, the importance of mechanisms that make sure that the input of citizens is then taken into account cannot be stressed enough. It would be very easy for large bureaucratic organizations to hold consultative forums in order to comply with regulations, but then to ignore the outcomes.

Publicly funded state broadcasting services could also contribute to a balanced deliberative debate. This could lead to the introduction of a real deliberative platform where representatives from all groups would receive equal airtime and equal respect. Of course, not all citizens are going to watch these programmes, but those who do could be exposed to different viewpoints as well as to the idea that those viewpoints should be respected equally. There is evidence that those who do so are also more likely to be opinion leaders who engage actively in civic duties (Scheufele and Shah 2000).

This brief list illustrates that there is already a wealth of deliberative institutions present in democratic societies. The first task of any serious deliberative democrat must be to strengthen these institutions rather than to re-design the entire political system to accommodate new ones. This would of course change the character of the deliberative democracy project. It would make it less ambitious, it would make it appear less ground-breaking, but at the same time it would also make it more realistic and easier to embrace for politicians who would have to legislate and implement reforms.

The question arises why such smaller-scale reforms have not already taken place and why there is no widespread call for such reforms. I believe the reason is that there is a lack of incentives for their introduction, both for politicians and citizens. Citizens have no interest or time to participate and would get relatively little benefit out of getting involved in political deliberation. Thus, we return to the problem of motivation. Most citizens would like democratic politics to function without intervention on their part, like a perpetuum mobile, producing good policy decisions; they underestimate the deep divisions that exist about policy matters and believe that politics would function very well without their help if only politicians and bureaucrats were not so inefficient, incompetent, selfish and removed from the reality of the wishes of ordinary people.

Yet liberal representative democracy appears to work more or less as intended, which means that neither politicians, nor citizens desire to change it drastically – especially if this requires increased effort on the part of citizens and increased risk for politicians. In order for deliberative initiatives to be successful, the case for deliberation needs to be very strong, both with respect to the theory and the practice of democratic deliberation.

7
Micro Deliberation in Practice

We have come a long way in the preceding six chapters. We have looked at what deliberative democracy is and discovered that defining this concept is a challenge in itself. We have examined the normative foundations of democratic theory, procedural values such as equality and inclusion, and seen how these apply to deliberative models of democracy. We have considered what reasoned deliberation means and whether it will lead to better decisions than other forms of democracy. We have also looked at whether we should expect deliberation to produce consensual decisions and how the theory can accommodate voting and bargaining. Finally, in the last chapter we looked at macro deliberation in practice and at some of the preconditions of introducing more deliberative practices into current democracies, not least the important condition of getting citizens motivated to participate.

While I have used empirical examples throughout, so far I have focused very much on the conceptual, theoretical side of things. In this chapter I will describe various forms of micro deliberative institution and evaluate them according to some of the normative criteria discussed earlier. These evaluations will of necessity be relatively brief; the aim of this chapter is not to provide an in-depth analysis of any of these institutions, which can be found elsewhere. Instead, this chapter will provide a general overview of how the theory of deliberative democracy has been applied to deliberation between citizens and how well these institutions conform to the normative standards of the literature.

Another reason why evaluation will often not be as in-depth as we might wish is that the data is simply missing. There are no studies that tell us whether internal inclusion is secured in citizens' juries and what the level of equality between participants in deliberative debate is. Most of the data relate to formal characteristics of the procedure, such as whether participant selection was inclusive, or whether there are appropriate rules in place that can secure equality.

As all of these deliberative forums are micro deliberative, they consist of face-to-face deliberation over a well-defined topic. The examples also involve citizens rather than politicians. Some of these forums have the power to achieve real change, others foster understanding and a deliberative spirit. I will start with the micro deliberative forum that is often taken as an archetype of democratic deliberation, but on closer inspection is probably nothing of the sort: New England town hall meetings.

Town Hall Meetings

The type of deliberative mini-publics that have existed by far the longest are the town hall meetings held in the United States. These meetings have taken place regularly since the seventeenth century in all municipalities of a number of New England states. They have been described by de Tocqueville as one of the principal ways in which the doctrine of sovereignty is applied in the US:

> [L]ocal assemblies of citizens constitute the strength of free nations. Town-meetings are to liberty what primary schools are to science; they bring it within the people's reach, they teach men how to use and how to enjoy it. A nation may establish a system of free government, but without the spirit of municipal institutions it cannot have the spirit of liberty. The transient passions and the interests of an hour, or the chance of circumstances, may have created the external forms of independence; but the despotic tendency which has been repelled will, sooner or later, inevitably reappear on the surface. (De Tocqeville, 1835/1945, chapter 5: 46)

Town hall meetings provide residents with a formal opportunity to deliberate together and make decisions regarding local issues that affect them directly, such as the maintenance of schools or roads.

While hundreds of such meetings take place every year in Connecticut, Massachusetts, Rhode Island, Maine, New Hampshire and Vermont, few detailed studies of these processes exist. Two exceptions are the qualitative study by Mansbridge (1980) of the Vermont town of 'Selby' and the quantitative study of Vermont town meetings carried out by Bryan (2004) over a period of thirty years.

Town hall meetings are often cited as a prime example of democratic deliberation. They encourage participation in debate aimed at making informed decisions directly relevant to the lives of the decision-makers. All registered voters in the area are formally entitled to attend. The fact that it is a community that makes a decision for itself can create feelings of solidarity and a drive for consensus. Mansbridge describes the town hall meetings she observed as mixed, both unitary and adversarial forms of local political decision making.

However, town meetings also fall short of the deliberative ideal in significant respects. Because they often take place in a relatively small community, personal differences and cleavages in that community become very important. The most common cleavages in the meetings studied by Mansbridge and Bryan include class differences, differences in education, a divide between those who live in the town and those who live in nearby rural areas, as well as between 'old-timers' and 'newcomers'. In a small community, participants can also feel that if they speak up they make a fool of themselves and are then laughed at and gossiped about for a long time (Mansbridge 1980). The cost of attending meetings can also differ greatly; if meetings are held on a workday, some residents might have to forgo a day's wages in order to attend.

As a result, Mansbridge argues that:

> In spite of the theoretically open character of the town meeting, the costs and benefits of attending are distributed in such a way that the old-timers, the villagers, the elderly, the middle class, and the self-confident are somewhat more likely to attend than neighbours. This means that when an issue comes to a vote these groups will have slightly more than their proportionate share of the votes. Since, in addition, they are more likely to be elected to town office, they will also be able to exercise disproportionate influence before and after the vote. (Mansbridge, 1980: 111)

Thus, even though it is readily embraced by deliberative democrats, the town hall meeting falls short of deliberative standards of inclusion and equality. Yet as a form of democratic deliberation, however imperfect, that has been successful over a long period of time and is run by the community it serves rather than by outside moderators or experts, it offers us a glimpse into what more organic forms of micro deliberation can look like.

Twenty-First Century Town Meetings, Citizens' Juries, Planning Cells and Consensus Conferences

Following in the wake of theories on participatory and deliberative democracy, the traditional town hall meeting format has been updated by America Speaks, a non-profit organization, under the name 'twenty-first century town meeting' (Fung 2003). These town meetings are just one example of a number of small-scale deliberative initiatives that are run at the behest of local governments and policymakers rather than as quasi-experiments. Other prominent examples are citizens' juries, planning cells and consensus conferences.

The twenty-first century town meeting's format was designed expressly along the lines of ideal deliberation. Its aim is to bring together a sample of citizens in larger cities and allow them to influence city government. In practice, this means that these town meetings are sponsored by city administrations and their feedback is often explicitly incorporated into future policy. This method can accommodate thousands of participants at a time by dividing them into groups of ten. Individual groups can feed their ideas back to the whole group and other small groups instantaneously through laptops distributed to tables. Participants also have the opportunity to vote on the recommendations they like the most.

Citizens' juries and planning cells were both developed in the 1970s. Citizens' juries were developed in the United States by Ned Crosby (Smith and Wales 2000; Crosby and Nethercut 2005), and they have been utilized in the UK, Spain and Australia, among other countries. Participants are selected through a system of stratified sampling that aims to pick a representative sample of the population based on age, gender, race, income and even political views. Between twelve and twenty-four jury members meet over a period of four to five days to discuss a predetermined topic. In order to increase the number of participants, sometimes multiple juries are run concurrently. The aim of organizers is to create a microcosm of the community that can engage in meaningful deliberation over weighty issues

(Crosby and Nethercut 2005). Citizens' juries make use of both expert witnesses and facilitators in order to make the discussion as informed and balanced as possible. While they were influential as a template for participatory democratic and deliberative processes, citizens' juries had a limited impact on actual political decisions.

Planning cells (*Planungszelle*) were invented in Germany by Peter Dienel (Hendriks 2005) and are predominantly used in that country, although they did exert an influence over citizens' juries introduced in countries such as the UK. They were originally designed to provide public input concerning municipal planning problems, for example, public transport development in Hamburg. Approximately 25 participants are selected through random sampling and are expected to participate in a process of deliberation that lasts for four days or a week. During the week citizens discuss issues both in small groups of five with a rotating membership and in larger sessions. In order to ensure a representative process, multiple planning cells are usually run on the same issue. While on average six to ten planning cells are run concurrently, this number can be as high as eighteen (Hendriks 2005).

Thus hundreds of citizens can participate in the process, albeit divided into smaller cells of 25. Each of these cells follows the same schedule of information sessions, expert testimonies and deliberative discussions and takes place with a minimal amount of facilitation. The output of small group discussions are recorded by 'process stewards' and this is used by the convenors to prepare a citizens' report once all cells have completed their work. Before the report is handed over to decision-makers the drafts are commented on by a member of each planning cell, thereby ensuring accountability in the report writing process.

Consensus conferences were developed in Denmark in the 1980s. Their aim was to provide decision-makers with a better understanding of the social context of new technologies and to stimulate public debate (Hendriks 2005). Twenty-five citizens are selected through a random sample to take place in a two-stage deliberative process, which is overseen by an external advisory committee. While the 25 citizens are lay persons, the advisory committee includes academics, experts and representatives of stakeholder groups. During the first stage participants draw up a list of questions to address and select expert witnesses that they want to hear evidence from. The second stage comprises the actual four-day deliberative conference. During

the conference the expert witnesses are called forward and participants deliberate among themselves with the help of facilitators. At
the end of the process a report is produced and presented to relevant
decision-makers.

These three schemes have some significant similarities. They are all
relatively small-scale initiatives that are usually commissioned by
local, regional or national government. All select participants through
some form of sampling, although citizens' juries use stratified
sampling and claim a higher degree of representativeness. They all rely
on the use of expert witnesses and only planning cells have a 'hands
off' approach to moderation. Consensus conferences stand out as they
allow more input from their participants in the agenda-setting process.

Importantly, these micro deliberative forums stand in stark
contrast to New England town hall meetings as they are almost
entirely top-down processes. These processes are initiated and their
cost is covered by administrative units which consult them in order to
learn about public attitudes and increase legitimacy. Their execution
relies heavily on experts and moderators. Their impact on the wider
public sphere varies. Danish consensus conferences are more widely
reported on, but the primary aim of the procedures is to inform
decision-makers and administrators rather than the public sphere. It
is notable that where multiple planning cells or citizens' juries are run
concurrently, their participants never meet formally in a plenary
session.

The remaining micro deliberative procedures discussed in this
chapter stand somewhere between the well-entrenched bottom-up
self-government of New England town hall meetings and these top-
down procedures.

Deliberative Polls

Deliberative polls have been designed and organized by researchers
and as a result they have been studied in greater detail than some of
the other initiatives discussed in this chapter (Fishkin 2009). They
also offer a useful source of data because unlike consensus conferences or participatory budgeting procedures, which have been modified between different localities to suit the needs of local organizers
better, deliberative polling has been conducted in a variety of countries in a more or less standardized format.

Deliberative polls are two-day events which, according to the Center for Deliberative Democracy at Stanford, aim to 'reveal the conclusions the public would reach, if people had opportunity to become more informed and more engaged by the issues' (Center for Deliberative Democracy 2012a). Polls have been held in many countries over diverse issues, such as the future of electric utilities in Texas, the future of the monarchy in Australia or discrimination against the Roma in Bulgaria. Even the Chinese Communist Party has sanctioned some deliberative experiments (He and Leib 2006). One of the latest polls was organized among citizens of different EU member states and was conducted with the help of translators (Center for Deliberative Democracy 2012b).

The participants of deliberative polls are selected using random number phone dialling or a random sampling of local phone numbers. Before they attend the deliberative weekend, they are asked to respond to a set of survey questions and to study a pack of balanced briefing materials provided by the organizers.

The actual deliberative event is divided into different phases. The bulk of the deliberative work takes place in small groups where all citizens are allowed equal time to have their say. These small groups feed back to plenary sessions, where group members have the opportunity to put questions to a panel of experts. There have been some attempts to provide wider publicity for the process and outcomes of these polls. As an example, the deliberative poll held on the UK national elections in 1997 has been televised on Channel 4.

Participants are surveyed both at the start and the end of the deliberative event. This data is the main source of research findings about the effectiveness of deliberative polls in changing citizen preferences. As we saw in Chapter 5, deliberative polls show an increase in meta-agreement, that is, deliberators are more likely to agree about the most important underlying issue dimension, even if they still disagree about the solution to that issue itself (List 2004; Farrar *et al.* 2010). Not surprisingly, deliberators are more likely to change their minds about issues which they know little about and on which they do not have any preconceived notions. Thus, they are more likely to change their opinion over energy policy or small business taxation than they are over the future of the monarchy in Australia. Fishkin and his team also found that individual preferences changed in a more other-regarding dimension, with participants more likely to feel compassion towards other members of society (Farrar *et al.* 2010). On the more negative side, post-survey polls have found that participants are still likely to have significant gaps in their factual knowledge, even after two days of discussion. But beyond the basic quantitative survey data, much richer findings could emerge from analyzing the content of the actual deliberative discussions themselves – work that is still underway.

A more ambitious version of deliberative polling is the idea of deliberation day (Ackermann and Fishkin 2004), which aims to introduce more deliberative institutions into national politics. Deliberation day would be held before national elections with the participation of every citizen, who would be remunerated for their efforts. Deliberative events following the format of deliberative polls would be held over two days in schools and community centres around the country, allowing citizens to hear each other's views, to question representatives of political parties and to cast better reasoned votes on election day.

This ambitious scheme shows us how the kind of bottom-up micro-deliberative initiatives discussed in this chapter could become a formal part of the wider political landscape. However, such a proposal would require vast resources: lost economic productivity from the days spent deliberating, running expenses and the cost of rewarding citizens for participating.

In their initial proposal, Ackermann and Fishkin developed deliberation day as a means for US citizens to get together before presidential elections and to discuss who would be best suited to lead the country next. But they extended the model to cover other elections as well, such as those for Congress and Senate in the US, and most recently the referendum on the EU constitution in Ireland (Ackermann and Fishkin 2008).

These deliberative polls show that it is possible to replicate a micro deliberative procedure based explicitly on the normative ideals of deliberative democracy across multiple countries and issues. What still remains to be established is that such procedures can have wider impact both on decision making and on macro deliberation in the public sphere.

Participatory Budgeting

Participatory budgeting (PB) procedures were first used in Porto Alegre, Brazil, in the 1980s, but have since then been extended to other Brazilian cities, other South American countries and many European countries including the UK (PB Unit 2012). Here I am going to focus on the original PB in Porto Alegre, as it has been running for the longest time and is thus the most well-established. PB is a very ambitious procedure that gives citizens exceptional powers over determining municipal project priorities and allocating funding. It also involves a large number of citizens, as attendances at some of the meetings can number thousands. The PB process has been highly influential in funding municipal projects, such as improved sanitation, transport or healthcare.

The PB is a year-round budgeting procedure that consists of a number of decision-making rounds that take place at various municipal decision-making levels. Porto Alegre is divided into sixteen districts, the sizes of which vary considerably from about 23,000 to 271,000 citizens (Gret and Sintomer 2005). Residents of all neighbourhoods are encouraged to organize into local neighbourhood associations with the aim of campaigning for specific local improvements, such as a new health centre or paved roads. The first step in the PB process involving the public consists of a series of local assemblies and forums where residents turn up to promote the projects of their neighbourhood associations, as well as a series of thematic assemblies that focus on issues affecting the entire city, such as education policy. These forums are well attended and thousands of citizens participate in them every year. It is here that delegates to the district forums are authorized. They are the leaders of neighbourhood associations and are selected based on the size and therefore prominence of their group.

It is in the district forums and the participatory budget council (COP) where most of the work takes place. Delegates to the district forums coordinate meetings, discuss budget priorities amongst themselves and with other district forums and appoint councillors to the highest citizen-led level of the budgeting procedure, the COP. This consists of two permanent councillors and two reserves from each of the sixteen district forums, the six thematic assemblies and the municipal executive, as well as one permanent and one reserve councillor from the two big public sector unions of Porto Alegre. Delegates and councillors are elected for one year and may not hold other public office. In the COP the previous and proposed budgets are reviewed and members of the COP work together closely with the city council in order to be able to evaluate and influence the budgetary process.

The budget is planned according to multiple criteria. Firstly, spending priorities discussed in the district forums and assemblies are largely determined by the number of people actively supporting each micro-local lobby group. Each district and thematic assembly selects four spending priorities, such as roads, sanitation or education. These thematic priorities are aggregated at the city level, determining city-wide spending priorities. It is these city-wide priorities, rather than the district-level priorities that will shape the final budget. Secondly, each district is assigned a grade to indicate how well it already performs in these areas and therefore which districts will need more spending than others. Thirdly, spending for each district is adjusted based on its population size.

One significant shortcoming of the PB process is the way in which the size of districts can affect spending decisions. Each district has the same number of delegates in the Council, therefore small districts will have the same amount of influence during deliberation as large districts with more diverse populations. The spending priorities selected at the district level are also weighted equally: the priorities of a populous district do not count for more when the city-wide priorities are selected than the priorities of a sparsely populated, semi-rural district.

Furthermore, district size is also a key variable when funding is allocated to projects. If road building is selected as one of the main city-wide thematic priorities for a year, a large district that already has a good road network and has not listed this as a development priority will nevertheless be assigned a part of the budget for it, simply based on the size of its population. But as far as overall investment goes, vastly unequal district sizes will lead to lower investment in districts with large populations, regardless of how poor or undeveloped those districts are, as the priorities of each district count equally, regardless of the number of residents.

Nevertheless, PB has proved successful in Porto Alegre for a relatively long period of time. While it may be less closely designed to follow the deliberative ideal than deliberative polling, it still represents a significant micro deliberative achievement. One question is whether this success is based on the fact that the budget allocation devised by PB and the participatory process itself is closely aligned with the aims of the left-wing PT party that has governed the city for most of this period (Cohen and Rogers 2003). There is little research-based evidence of the success of PB in other countries, therefore it is difficult to tell how effective these procedures are in different settings. I can, however, offer some anecdotal evident from my own experience. The local council in the UK where I live organized a PB process in 2009, but this was so poorly publicized despite a large budget, that I only found out about it after it has taken place, even though I have significant personal and professional interest in micro deliberation.

British Columbia Citizens' Assembly

Citizens of British Columbia were asked by their government to participate in a unique project in 2004 (Warren and Pearse 2008). By participating in a month-long deliberative process they got to choose how the electoral system of British Columbia could be improved. Their suggestion for changing the current majority rule system to a single transferable vote (STV) system was then put to citizens in a referendum held at the same time as the next elections. The process had very significant support from the state government and generous funding.

Participants were selected from all districts of British Columbia through the use of stratified sampling. This gave the Assembly a claim to representativeness. Two native American deliberators were added at the last moment when it became clear that the group had no aboriginal members.

Before deliberations started participants spent six weeks learning about various electoral systems and the deliberative process itself. After this, panels of deliberators attended public hearings held all over British Columbia as well as receiving a large number of written contributions from members of the public. Only then, after months of preparatory work, did the actual deliberative process start. Deliberators held discussions both in small groups and in plenary sessions and had the support of academic experts throughout.

Citizens were first asked to decide on the three most important criteria for choosing an electoral system. They chose *effective local representation, proportionality* and *maximizing voter choice*. Deliberators then evaluated electoral systems according to how well they performed against these criteria. This narrowed the discussion down to two electoral systems: mixed member proportional representation (MMP) and STV. During the final stage of deliberation citizens made pair-wise comparisons between MMP, STV and the existing single-member majority rule system. They chose STV over MMP and decided that STV was preferable to the existing system, thereby allowing the government to put a concrete recommendation to voters in the upcoming referendum.

One major shortcoming of the process was the lack of publicity. No official 'yes' and 'no' campaigns were run before the referendum and most citizens were unaware that they would not only be making use of the electoral system on polling day, but also voting on whether to alter it (Smith 2009). However, citizens who were aware of the work of Citizens' Assembly found their recommendations trustworthy and the majority of them were prepared to vote 'yes' in the referendum (Cutler *et al.* 2008). Deliberators from the Assembly participated in local forums where they explained the reasoning behind their choice to voters, which did provide some help with making the voters better informed.

The eventual failure of the referendum illustrates that even significant government support, investment of time and resources and good organization are still not sufficient to provide a wider impact for micro deliberation without linking that process to deliberation in the wider public sphere.

Further Procedures

While the above is just a small selection of some of the most prominent micro deliberative procedures, it offers a good overview of those currently in use. However, there are some other institutions that are still worth mentioning, however briefly.

Some of these remaining institutions are micro deliberative forums that involve the users of local government services such as schools, healthcare providers or the police. A good example is provided by the two types of community deliberation Fung (2004) has studied in Chicago: local school councils and an alternative, community-supported policing strategy. Both of these micro deliberative institutions have the support of the city government and are therefore able to lead to real change. They deal with local services that are vital to residents and aim to empower them through giving them a say in how those services are run.

National issues forums are special, in that their aim is to simply generate wider deliberation among the general public and greater awareness and understanding of difficult issues, without any obvious feedback mechanism to policy-makers. The forums are organized by a wide range of organizations: libraries, schools, churches, senior groups, prisons or businesses. Training for moderators and convenors is provided by the National Issues Forum Institute in the United States. The Institute also provides nonpartisan deliberation materials developed by the Kettering Foundation on a wide range of public policy topics and continues to develop more of them as a response to current issues. This format can be viewed as an element within the wider context of public sphere deliberation.

Despite the costliness of such endeavours, micro deliberative forums other than deliberative polls are also organized by researchers. One prominent recent example is the 2009 Australian Citizens' Parliament, which brought together 150 citizens to generate recommendations for reforming the Australian system of governance. Participants were selected using stratified sampling. The process, which was based on the twenty-first century town hall model, consisted of multiple stages. Citizens participated in local meetings and in online discussion before meeting in the Old Parliament building in Canberra for four days of deliberation. The venue of the Citizens' Parliament added to the gravity of the process. Over the four days both small- and large-group discussions took place under the supervision of moderators. The Citizens' Parliament has been successful at providing a number of recommendations and has received overwhelmingly positive feedback from its participants (New Democracy 2009). Recommendations included harmonizing laws across Australian state boundaries, empowering citizens to participate in politics more and changing the voting system to optional preferential voting.

In addition to any immediate benefits to citizen participants, the Citizens' Parliament has also provided a rich set of data for current and future research projects. This includes four sets of survey data charting the preferences and attitudes at various stages of the process as well as audio recordings of the actual deliberation. While the Citizens' Parliament has been a success, it is worth noting that about 200 staff were needed to organize the event. Thus such relatively large-scale deliberative events take a large amount of resources to set up.

Evaluation

These micro deliberative institutions have enough in common for us to be able to evaluate them together based on the normative criteria that have been discussed in previous chapters. This serves two important purposes. First, it allows us to test some of the theoretical assumptions we have made. Second, it gives us an overview of the most important strengths and weaknesses, threats and opportunities when thinking about the design of micro deliberative institutions.

Agenda setting and transparency

While it is ordinary citizens who do the actual deliberating in micro deliberative forums, they do so within the constraints of a process that has been designed by others. In most of these processes, issues and questions are defined in advance, the sequencing of events is decided on and experts are selected by organizers. This means that those commissioning and running these events have agenda-setting powers that can have a direct influence on the outcome of the procedure.

During the British Columbia Citizens' Assembly (BCCA) some participants felt dissatisfied with the way in which the organizers influenced the outcome, for example by requiring them to limit the number of priorities against which voting systems were evaluated to three (Lang 2008). Arguably, the outcome could have looked quite different if more priorities had been allowed.

While the participatory budgeting procedure is regularly reviewed and revised by its participants, and it is citizens who set the main spending priorities, full-time employees of the city hall still have a significant role in shaping the final outcome (Gret and Sintomer 2005). The formula according to which the budget is allocated relies not only on the preferences of residents, but also on an evaluation of needs carried out by experts.

Consensus conferences include an important first step to freer agenda setting by allowing participants to select the most important questions to be addressed and the expert witnesses to be summoned, albeit with the help of a board of expert advisers. But in most micro deliberative forums the agenda-setting powers of participants is very limited.

Submitting collective choices to deliberation is not sufficient to achieve legitimacy. As we have seen in Chapters 2 and 5, democratic deliberation is part of a wider democratic system of decision making. Thus, transparency about when and why micro deliberative forums are organized, and at times even more importantly, why they are not, is necessary. It is also necessary that there should be an ongoing dialogue between the participants of deliberative and non-deliberative modes of decision making. For this, feedback mechanisms need to be in place that allow administrators to tell deliberators how their decisions were implemented or passed on to other decision-making bodies, as well as allowing for feedback from the deliberators themselves about how the deliberative process could be improved. Currently, with the notable exceptions of town hall meetings and PB, micro deliberative forums are organized on an ad hoc basis, making such transparency hard to achieve.

Group size and inclusion

Studies of micro deliberative processes underline the fact that the most effective deliberation happens in small groups rather than large ones. The organizers of citizens' juries, consensus conferences and planning cells have opted for having multiple, smaller groups that never meet; other deliberative events rely on citizens separating into smaller groups between plenary sessions. The reason for this is simple: the larger the group, the fewer people can talk and for shorter periods of time (Dahl, 2006). If deliberation goes on for six hours in a group of ten, each participant has thirty-six minutes to speak, in a group of fifty just over seven minutes, in a group of a hundred around three and a half minutes, and in a group of five hundred people speaking time per person is reduced to under a minute. And these figures do not take into account periods of silence.

This reflects a problem that participatory models of democracy face if they are extended beyond the strictly local, workplace or family level. The most famous participatory democracy of all, the ancient Athenian city state, illustrates this example well. While all citizens participated in public assemblies, only a small minority of them actually spoke in public (Ober 2008). Furthermore, even these public assemblies excluded women, slaves and immigrants, thereby further restricting the size of the demos.

In his study of town hall meetings Bryan (2004) also finds size important for participation. Using data from town meetings in Vermont over a period of 30 years, he finds that as the number of residents in a town increases, the proportion who participate in town meetings decreases sharply. Equally, as the number of those present at a town meeting increases, the number of those who talk decreases sharply.

This highlights one of the key limitations of these kind of micro deliberative processes, namely that relatively few citizens will be able to participate in them productively. This increases the importance of participant selection for ensuring external inclusion (Young 2000). Even stratified sampling cannot guarantee that all affected individuals will be sufficiently represented. The organizers of the BCCA found that they needed to specially invite two Aboriginal deliberators to ensure an Aboriginal presence, and even after this intervention, women, those of lower education and ethnic minorities were under-represented (Warren and Pearse 2008).

While most of these micro deliberative procedures try to ensure fair and inclusive participant selection through the use of random or stratified sampling techniques, there always remains an element of self-selection; as it is not compulsory to attend, those who are most interested are the more likely to come along. These may be people who have the most to gain or lose, those most interested in politics or most civic-minded.

Furthermore, we need to view levels of participation in micro deliberative events within the context of general political participation. While women are under-represented in the PB process, their numbers compare favourably with the rates of participation in Brazilian government in general (Gret and Sintomer 2005).

Even if external inclusion is secured, the thorny issue of ensuring internal inclusion during the actual debate remains. Both Mansbridge (1980) and Bryan (2004) report instances of exclusion during debates in their studies of town hall meetings. Bryan records an especially common version of this exclusion: that of the tension between insiders and outsiders. Old-time residents of small localities in Vermont often sidelined newcomers, whom they regarded as city-dwellers who could not appreciate the nuances of the local community.

It appears that the more formalized micro deliberation is, the less of a problem internal exclusion presents, possibly due to better-defined rules and the presence of moderators. Participants of the elected deliberative council in Porto Alegre reported that even those who were inexperienced, poor or possessed relatively low levels of formal education were included and supported by other members of their group. Deliberative polls use maximum speaking times and moderators to ensure fair participation. But even such methods will have to face up to the problems of substantive equality discussed in Chapter 4; not all will be equally persuasive during a deliberative debate, no matter what formal rules we introduce to facilitate inclusion.

Commitment

Most of these initiatives take place over a relatively short period of time. As the citizens' jury and planning cell methods developed over time, organizers found that at least four days of hearing evidence and discussions were needed in order for citizens to be able to make a well-informed decision, but at the same time citizens would have been much less willing to participate if the process took more than one week (Crosby and Nethercut 2005). Deliberative polls claim to achieve informed deliberation on issues over the course of just a weekend.

The two notable exceptions are PB and the BCCA, both of which take place over a significantly longer period of time. Even though the BCCA regularly required the services of citizens for a number of months, it was a one-off event. While the PB not only requires regular participation, but is also a recurring process, in practice councillors are limited to a two-year term and the evidence suggests that the attendees at public meetings change over time (Smith 2009).

While participants reported a great deal of enthusiasm in participating in these deliberative events, this was to a significant degree due to the fact that they saw themselves as privileged by being able to participate in a one-off deliberative exercise. If public deliberation became more common and citizens were able to or were required to take part more than once in their lifetime, these attitudes might change. Furthermore, even though most of these initiatives use some form of statistical sampling to ensure fair access and that a representative sample of the population is selected, they still rely to some extent on self-selection, as not all of those initially invited will be willing to take part.

Motivation can of course be provided from sources other than civic duty. One common incentive offered to participants is monetary remuneration in exchange for participating in deliberation. Ackermann and Fishkin (2004) propose to pay each citizen $100 in return for fulfilling their civic duty. Experiments with human subjects, whether in medicine, psychology or the social sciences, often use cash as an incentive to attract participants and the organizers of focus groups and opinion polls regularly offer cash incentives or shopping vouchers to participants. Similarly, deliberative polls have also offered small sums to those who attended meetings. Anecdotal evidence confirms that these payments are very important to participants. Organizers of one deliberative event received numerous phone calls before payments were processed from people anxious to receive their money.

Being paid to do their civic duty clearly encourages people to participate. However, this strategy may lead to bias in participant selection, just as self-selection without such incentives did. Firstly, cash rewards are more likely to attract poorer members of society: the unemployed, pensioners, those on low incomes. This may not be a problem if these groups are otherwise under-represented in the political process. In the case of deliberation day, which would be a national holiday, it is not difficult to see that many citizens may decide that a day off is worth more than $100.

Secondly, the organizers of deliberative events can also motivate people to attend through lowering the cost of doing so. A common problem for parents is the lack of availability and the cost of childcare. This can easily be remedied by the provision of a professionally run crèche service. Participants could also be reimbursed for transport or childcare costs and free on-site meals could be provided. Incidentally, meals, coffee breaks, common transport and childcare arrangements could also encourage the small talk that I have argued in Chapter 4 is essential for successful deliberation.

Impact

As we saw in the previous chapter, in order for citizens to be motivated to attend deliberative events, they need to see that their participation has a direct and palpable impact on actual policy (Cohen and Rogers 2003). More than anything else, this can make the difference between citizens viewing deliberation as an important part of their civic duty or simply a waste of time.

The impact that citizen-led micro deliberative events have on policy outcomes varies widely. At one end of the spectrum, the aim of National Issues Forums and study circles is to inform and mobilize citizens, rather than to change policy. At the other end of the spectrum, participatory budgeting procedures, the BCCA and some of the deliberative polls were essential in shaping outcomes. This is especially true for participatory budgeting procedures, which, while not formalized in law, are part of the official decision-making process. The outcome of the BCCA, by contrast, had to be ratified through a referendum. Deliberation in legislatures and executives, on the other hand, has always been key to political decision making.

Most of the procedures discussed in this chapter, however, will only on occasion make an impact on actual policy. Even if these processes reveal what decision citizens would make if they were well-informed and gave issues serious thought, the difficulty lies in convincing politicians to take the outcomes seriously and to transmit those outcomes to the wider electorate.

If procedures have less impact than participants initially expected, this can lead to disillusionment with the process. This highlights the need for transparency about all aspects of the deliberative process.

The influence of the deliberative procedure also depends on the publicity it receives. As noted earlier, the BCCA received relatively little publicity and this may have contributed to the failure of the referendum proposal to change the electoral system. The impact of citizens' juries, consensus conferences and planning cells also appears to be linked to the extent to which the story is picked up by the media. Media coverage is also important in fulfilling one of the main objectives of micro deliberation, as it transmits the results of the process to citizens who did not participate and thereby fosters debate around the issue in the wider public sphere. The difficulty is that micro deliberation is not naturally suited to media coverage (Smith 2009). The process takes place over long periods of time and hinges on detailed and reasoned discussion. This fits uneasily with the 24-hour news cycle and with shorter, edited programmes and news coverage that focuses on conflict and spectacle. Therefore, coverage of deliberative polls tended to focus on the expert witnesses and recognizable names rather than the dialogue between ordinary citizens.

Another potential impact of citizen participation in micro deliberation is that those citizens would then be more likely to participate in macro deliberation in the public sphere. There are as yet no research findings that indicate if this is the case or not. The only conclusion that can be drawn regarding the impact of micro deliberative procedures

organized among ordinary citizens is that without wide-ranging institutional change their impact will remain limited.

Conclusion

This chapter has shown that there is wide variation among contemporary micro deliberative practices. New England town hall meetings
have by far the longest history and are truly local events organized
from the bottom up. Others, such as citizens' juries and deliberative
polls, have been developed as innovative ways of influencing public
policy. While the institutions discussed in this chapter are all different
we can still evaluate them against the framework developed earlier in
this book.

While actual micro deliberative procedures do fulfill some of the
normative values of the ideal theory, they do so in a piecemeal fashion. They may generate real deliberation, but only among a small
group of self-selected citizens. Town hall meetings give everyone an
equal right to attend, but not everyone is treated equally at the meetings. They may be inclusive in their participant selection, but then
produce very limited impact on actual policy. The application of the
theory of deliberative democracy to such small-scale forums is still in
its infancy. The best way forward may be to identify the strength of
each procedure and construct a theory of best practice out of these –
work that is yet to be done.

8
Conclusion

This final chapter draws together the debates analyzed in the book. It will address two key questions raised in earlier chapters. The first concerns the reasons for holding deliberative democracy to be valuable, while the second concerns the problems inherent in a democratic theory based primarily on deliberation.

Contemporary democratic theory puts deliberation of one form or another centre stage. As we have seen, there are good reasons for valuing democratic deliberation. However deliberation is favoured at the cost of neglecting other valuable components of the democratic decision-making process. During deliberation, participants are expected to change their beliefs and preferences following new information and good arguments, thereby ideally leading to the victory of the best argument. Setting aside the question of whether a best argument can truly exist among competing reasonable viewpoints, this assumption ignores the crucial insight that most political debates are concerned either with the distribution of scarce resources amongst competing parties or with issues on which individuals have very deeply held, conflicting moral beliefs. Assuming that beliefs and preferences can be readily changed over these issues ignores the fundamental nature of these questions and shows insufficient respect for individuals' views. When it comes to competition for scarce resources, especially in cases where considerations of justice cannot be straightforwardly applied, bargaining may prove to be an acceptable way of making decisions. Similarly, when we need to make decisions that draw on deeply held, reasonable moral beliefs, fair and equal methods of voting may be appropriate. Therefore, a legitimate democratic process needs not only deliberation, but also other forms of political behaviour, such as voting, bargaining and protest.

All of this should influence the direction that the theory of deliberative democracy and more broadly, democratic theory could and should take in the future. With the growth of the empirical literature on democratic deliberation, political theorists need to respond to problems that these studies raise for the theoretical model. Furthermore, as the model of deliberative democracy becomes more sophisticated, there is an increasing trend to look at democratic deliberation within a system of public spheres and within a wider process of democratic decision making, rather than just in ideal and formal settings.

These developments have to be considered in relation to other theories of democracy which compete with the deliberative model. While there are no strong competitors in contemporary democratic theory, there are potential challenges from integrating the theory of deliberative democracy with theories of democratic representation and in clarifying the position of deliberative democracy with respect to both participatory and elite models of democracy.

Why Deliberation is Ultimately Desirable

The desirability of any theory of democracy depends both on the normative values underlying it and the mechanisms it offers for actualizing those values. We are now in a position to look at the values most crucial to the theory of deliberative democracy and see where the greatest strength of the theory lies.

In Chapter 4 I examined what are perhaps the most attractive values offered to justify deliberative democracy procedurally: inclusion and equality. These two are also at the heart of what can make deliberation democratic. Ideal deliberation should include all affected citizens and relevant arguments and give everyone equal influence over the procedure. This is clearly not the case in current political life, and deliberative democrats do not offer us strong mechanisms to ensure that it will be the case in a more deliberative democracy. Yet if inclusion and equality cannot be ensured, the legitimacy of deliberation cannot derive from these two values.

While in Chapter 3 I argued that we need to be cautious about endorsing an epistemic justification of deliberative democracy, the key to the value of democratic deliberation may still lie in the principle of decision making through well reasoned, other-regarding debate. After all, one of the major normative appeals of deliberative democracy is that it captures our intuition that political decisions that affect a large number of people, if not the entire society, need to be considered carefully. We must devote sufficient time and attention to such policies. We should discuss them and not make hasty or arbitrary choices.

This is due to the special nature of political decisions: they are unavoidably *collective*. Political decisions deeply affect the lives of many citizens and determine how the state will treat individuals. Given that in the democratic polity the state embodies the people, political decisions are decisions about how citizens ought to treat each other. Thus they have an important moral and ethical component and are essential for the constitution of a just society.

Furthermore, these decisions have to be made collectively, because the goods that the decisions are concerned with are also collective (Christiano 1996, 2004). It makes no sense for individuals or groups in society to decide on welfare policies, policing and security policies or environmental policies on their own. Christiano (1996: 59–62) sets out four conditions that goods need to satisfy in order to count as a collective property of society. First, they need to be *non-exclusive*: it is not possible for them to affect a person's life without affecting the lives of others. Pollution, the condition of roads or wars are all non-exclusive in this sense. Second, collective properties are *public,* that is, they only include issues that affect the welfare of everyone. Some citizens may hold meddlesome preferences over some issues even if these do not affect their welfare, but this does not suffice to make these the subject of collective decision making. Third, sharing these collective properties is *inevitable*: we all live together on a relatively small area of the planet, breathing the same polluted or clean air. Finally, the properties of a collective good need to be *alterable*; it makes no sense to try to make public decisions about them if they are not.

The fact that these decisions have to be made collectively and will affect our lives collectively, for better or for worse, makes them very different from private decisions. As they often affect a large number of people with diverse interests, we need to consider their effects on others carefully. Furthermore, collective decisions must not be arbitrary, benefiting some and harming others without good reason.

These collective decisions have to be made under conditions of pluralism. Citizens will hold a variety of reasonable, but often conflicting beliefs and preferences. These viewpoints need to be reconciled in any political decision in a way that is ideally acceptable to all, or nearly all reasonable persons. Some of these decisions may need to be made collectively at the national level, some may even need to be made at the global level, but many of these collective issues can be decided on the level of the local community.

Thus the primary value of deliberation may be that it allows for deep, meaningful reflection before collective decisions are taken. This has more to do with the time and effort that we spend on deliberation than expectations that it will transform preferences in a certain way or that it fosters equality or inclusion, since as we have seen in earlier chapters each of these assumptions is problematic in its own way. At the same time, many of the procedural values of the theory of deliberative democracy may still be necessary if we want to give collective decisions the necessary weight and importance across the entire society.

But the fact that such collective decisions are of special importance and that they should be considered carefully does not yet necessarily point us towards deliberative democracy. After all, Rousseau argued against long-drawn-out discussion as he believed that it would encourage factionality, partial interest and dissent (Rousseau 1997; Urbinati 2006). It is only yet another intuition that leads us to talking to each other in a reasoned manner in order to reach a decision. This is the intuition that political discussion will lead to a better understanding of each other and of issues, a greater willingness to be other-regarding and to do the right thing, as well as leading to decisions that are acceptable to all, even the losers.

Deciding collective matters through deliberation also seems to be a very academic intuition, applying similar standards to weighty decisions in the public sphere that we would apply to weighty matters in the seminar room. Thus, we need to consider whether this intuition really applies. Having examined the different justifications of deliberative democracy as well as many of its practical and theoretical limitations, we are now in a position to do just this.

Problems with the Deliberative Conception of Politics

There are two main types of criticism that we can make against deliberative democracy: pragmatic and normative. *Pragmatic* criticisms centre on the problems of implementing and sustaining deliberative democracy in real-world politics. Deliberative democrats acknowledge that we can never achieve ideal political deliberation, where deliberators face no time constraints, all have equal power and influence, citizens reason perfectly and are perfectly well-informed. Nevertheless, they also hold that this ideal can be approximated sufficiently in real-world political processes in order for us to enjoy the normative benefits of deliberation. Practical criticisms of deliberation suggest that this is not the case and furthermore, even if it was, the costs of implementation would far outweigh the benefits.

Normative criticisms, on the other hand, state that not only do we face pragmatic problems in achieving the kind of deliberation that the theory calls for, but that even if we could achieve this, it would in fact not be normatively desirable. As for much of the book, I will continue to focus on normative criticisms here.

We can now see that the theory of deliberative democracy assumes the existence of a very specific normative conception of politics. This conception wants to honour the seriousness of collective decisions and it wants to do so by making collective decision making more reasoned and more mutual. However, there are three problems with such a conception of politics. Firstly, the kind of debate favoured by deliberative democrats often seems apolitical in nature. Focusing on reasoned discussion and preference transformation in line with the deliberative ideal leads to a relative neglect of citizens' interests and strongly held moral and ethical beliefs. Secondly, deliberative democrats make very specific assumptions about which viewpoints count as reasonable, how preferences will be transformed and what kind of outcomes they will result in. Thirdly, as we have seen repeatedly over the previous chapters, participating in deliberative democracy is very costly, which creates problems for those who do not agree with the deliberative conception of politics. As a result, deliberation cannot be used as the main decision-making method and the foundation of a model of democracy.

My first charge is that deliberative democracy is apolitical. Deliberative democrats do not require citizens to put aside their own interests and preferences entirely (Mansbridge *et al.* 2010). They argue that it is acceptable to introduce our interests into the discussion as one of the factors which everyone should take into account when decisions are made, but ultimately we should not base our final collective decision only on each citizen's selfish private interests. This still requires them to adopt a specific frame when it comes to collective goods, one that is not only tolerant of others, but also other-regarding, seeking to take the needs of others into account when choices are made. This is a view of politics where self-interest is less important than making decisions that are mutually not only acceptable, but appear to be good for other participants.

Difference democrats, most notably Young (2000), have of course pointed out that one of the problems with the standard model of deliberative democracy is that it favours dispassionate, logical debate of the form traditionally practised among well-educated white males, thereby putting everyone else, including women, minorities, and the not so well-educated at a disadvantage. The solution Young offers to this problem is shifting the focus from 'deliberation', a conceptually loaded term that reminds us of the seminar room more than it does of politics, to 'communication'. Communication includes more ways of exchanging information than deliberation does, and communicative democracy puts a special emphasis on inclusion. The rough reasoning is that by including more forms of communication, we will also include more people. However, this does not solve the fundamental problem that frequently deliberation will not be the best way of solving collective problems, as it is apolitical and does not accommodate the magnitude of disagreement between citizens.

Politics is founded on disagreement over moral issues as well as on disagreement about allocating scarce resources. As we have seen above, this leads us to desire a political process that gives proper weight to collective decisions. But at the same time, it should also lead us to seek a political system that takes into account people's interests, as well as the very strong beliefs that they hold over some issues such as abortion, wars or the environment. Sometimes the strength of people's interests and beliefs will preclude the kind of benign, apolitical discussion that deliberation must be in order to remain reasoned and other-regarding. Instead they will need political opportunities that will allow these interests to be expressed and reconciled and solutions to be found without asking citizens to compromise on the strength of their preferences or beliefs. For these reasons, bargaining and interest group politics are often better ways of resolving democratic conflict.

The second problem is that the model of deliberative democracy makes important assumptions about the types of beliefs and preferences reasonable individuals will hold and the way these will be transformed.

At times the model of deliberative democracy does not accommodate viewpoints which do not correspond to the conception of politics that it portrays. Thus, Gutmann and Thompson (1996) reject
viewpoints that they consider irrational on the basis that they are
weakly grounded in morality. Arguments they disagree with are clas-
sified as 'unreasonable' or not 'moral reasons'. Stanley Fish notes the
following about Gutmann and Thompson's treatment of the parents
in the *Mozert v Hawkins Board of Education* case, who objected to the
use of certain textbooks on religious grounds: 'Notice that what
looks like an argument is really a succession of dismissive gestures
designed to deflect objections to a position [Gutmann and
Thompson] are unwilling to relinquish or even examine. Ironically,
these gestures are the best example of the closed-mindedness the
authors inveigh against' (Fish 1999: 91). Close-minded is too strong a
word for the position of most deliberative democrats when it comes to
deciding which types of preferences are reasonable and sufficiently
other-regarding, but there is certainly a worrying trend towards
assuming away opposition viewpoints that clash with the ethos of
deliberation.

Furthermore, the deliberative process does not just aggregate individual views and preferences. The outcomes that emerge out of
discussion are more than the sum of their parts and instead they are
the result of a collective transformation of preferences. This partly
explains the repeated emphasis on consensus, that the decisions made
through deliberation are somehow more agreeable to each individual
than a simple compromise, because they are the result of this collective and valuable process.

Of course this means that we have to make the assumption that the
deliberative procedure results in the right kind of preference transformation. Deliberative democrats rely on the argument that if citizens
get together to deliberate, they will do so in a civil manner and will
increasingly come to adopt other-regarding preferences. As their
preferences are transformed, as they create shared meaning out of
their discussion with other groups, they will produce a collective decision that is qualitatively different from decisions produced through
non-deliberative means, such as interest group and electoral politics.

Experience tells us, and the social sciences confirm, that social and
political life is often not like this. Instead, people often define themselves in opposition to others and use perspectives that are not other-
regarding, or at least not when it comes to those whom they do not

regard as 'one of them'. Politics is often highly adversarial. Citizens have interests and beliefs and are often willing to fight for them, rather than assessing the needs of others.

The problem with the theory of deliberative democracy is that when it argues that more political decisions should be made through discussion between citizens, it also defines how those discussions should take place and what kind of outcomes they should result in. Or even more problematically, the literature sometimes prescribes how those discussions should take place in order to arrive at an outcome which the theorists hold to be desirable. But we cannot even usually agree on how to fulfill the values that deliberative democracy advocates. One person's other-regarding policy may be another person's selfish, misguided one. Welfare policies are a prime example of this.

The third problem is that, as we have seen above, participating in deliberation is a very costly activity. In the theory, this participation becomes the civic duty of citizens, but at no point is this assumed to be burdensome. However, we cannot assume that all citizens will hold a conception of the 'political' that allows for this. Many citizens will view politics as something which does not require active participation on their part, as something irrelevant, or as something that is fundamentally rooted in strong moral claims or conflict. This is born out by evidence from surveys both from the US (Verba *et al.* 1995) and the UK (Electoral Commission 2006, 2007, 2011).

As we have seen above, the amount and kind of political participation that is required by the theory of deliberative democracy will limit the freedom of citizens. Of course, even the most minimal conceptions of the political will restrict this freedom to some extent, but the deliberative conception of politics will do so more than, let us say, the current liberal representative one. The reason for this is that it requires very specific standards of deliberative political behaviour that are costly both in terms of time and resources and psychologically, by requiring citizens to be other-regarding and practise reciprocity.

Citizens, however, cannot have a duty to participate in politics to an extent that interferes with their other opportunities and interests. This violates their liberty to choose what their idea of the good life is. While in general participation in democratic politics is better viewed as a right rather than a duty (Lever 2010, Brennan 2011), the argument that voting should be considered a minimal duty for citizens is more plausible, as it contributes to the checks and balances and the upkeep of a political system – liberal representative democracy – that allows them to live freely and to choose their own conception of the good life. Deliberation does not do this. Inasmuch as the state forces citizens to participate in deliberation, it tells them that the good life is one where everyone participates in political life extensively.

This means that making deliberation compulsory would impinge on citizens' freedom to participate as little or as much in politics as they want to. While some have made an argument for compulsory voting (Lever 2010), these arguments will not hold given the cost of deliberation for individuals. And as I argued in Chapter 4 (see page 79), some citizens, such as the Amish or Trotskyists, hold a conception of politics or the good life which is opposed to participation in deliberation. If only a few citizens would want to take part in deliberative exercises, the only possibility is to ensure participation through coercion. This violates the principle of political liberty.

However, if deliberation is not compulsory, it is more likely to become biased. There is a statistically significant relationship between participation in political activities and socio-economic background (Verba *et al.* 1995). Better-educated, wealthier citizens are not only more likely to vote, but they are also more likely to participate in other forms of political activity, such as campaigning for parties and candidates. A similar bias could develop in the case of deliberation as well. This would decrease the legitimacy of deliberative decisions significantly. We cannot argue that a community, a society or the electorate decided an issue through deliberative discussion when in fact a biased subgroup of it has done so. This is especially true as those who hold intense preferences over issues are also more likely to participate in deliberation. These participants are unlikely to change their preferences drastically as a result of hearing new arguments during deliberation, as they already have strong beliefs and preferences over the issue in question. Such biased deliberation does not correspond to the normative standards laid out in the deliberative democracy literature. And such imperfect deliberation also raises questions about other normative issues, such as equality or legitimacy, which could threaten the deliberative democracy project.

As a result of these problems, deliberation must be seen not as the ultimate foundation of democratic politics, but as one element among many in political decision making. Other elements are necessary for a healthy democracy. Bargaining is often necessary to resolve interest group politics. High emotions and strong beliefs are manifested through protests and demonstrations. Citizens are relieved of day-to-day political decision making through delegation to elected representatives and career bureaucrats.

One can now raise the objection that no deliberative democrat ignores the continued need for elections and representation and other forms of political action. However, they do argue that deliberation is at the very least the first among equals. While these other aspects of political life may be necessary too, it is deliberation that should be the legitimating driving force in democratic regimes, since it connects citizens and politicians in a framework of moral policy making and it should be the basis on which other decision-making mechanisms, such as bargaining, are legitimized.

But deliberation is unable to achieve this function. As we have seen, the justifications offered for it are not strong enough and the kind of conception of politics that it favours is too participatory and too apolitical to be the best one in a pluralistic society. Instead, democratic politics needs to be viewed as a more complex system of interactions. One of these is deliberation, and while it is important, it is not more important than other mechanisms such as representation or interest group politics.

Democratic theory needs to recognize that a legitimate democratic process needs not only deliberation, but also other forms of political behaviour, such as voting, bargaining and protest. In addition, we need to take greater account of the fact that in large contemporary democracies we cannot escape the need for political representation. We need to consider these aspects of democratic decision making and particularly the ways in which they interact with each other, possibly forming hybrid modes of political action, such as a mix of deliberation and bargaining. And we need to develop plausible standards for these types of political behaviour, especially in the light of social inequalities and inequalities in power. In addressing such issues, we may credibly extend the theory of democracy beyond the current deliberative model.

Recommended Reading

Monographs

Christiano, Thomas (1996) *The Rule of the Many: Fundamental Issues in Democratic Theory* (Boulder, CO: Westview Press): offers strong foundations for an intrinsic justification of deliberative democracy.

Dryzek, John S. (2000) *Deliberative Democracy and Beyond: Liberals, Critics, Contestations* (Oxford: Oxford University Press): a comprehensive theory of deliberative democracy from a critical theory perspective.

Dryzek, John S. (2006) *Deliberative Global Politics* (Oxford: Polity): applies Dryzek's theory of discursive democracy to global level deliberation.

Dryzek, John S. (2010) *Foundations and Frontiers of Deliberative Governance* (Oxford: Oxford University Press): addresses questions raised by the further development of the theory of deliberative democracy.

Estlund, David (2008) *Democratic Authority: A Philosophical Framework* (Princeton, NJ: Princeton University Press): a defence of democracy (in particular deliberative democracy) based on epistemic proceduralism.

Goodin, Robert (2008) *Innovating Democracy: Democratic Theory and Practice After the Deliberative Turn* (Oxford: Oxford University Press): a critique of recent developments in the theory and practice of deliberative democracy.

Gutmann, Amy and Dennis Thompson (1996) *Democracy and Disagreement* (Cambridge, MA: Belknap Press): the book develops one of the first detailed theories of deliberative democracy and applies it to a range of public policy issues.

Fishkin, James (2009) *When the People Speak: Deliberative Democracy and Public Consultation* (Oxford: Oxford University Press): a comprehensive description of the theory behind deliberative polling.

Habermas, Jürgen (1996) *Between Facts And Norms: Contributions to a Discourse Theory of Law and Democracy* (Oxford: Polity): offers a philosophical basis for the theory of deliberative democracy.

Smith, Graham (2009) *Democratic Innovations: Designing Institutions for Citizen Participation* (Cambridge: Cambridge University Press): a comprehensive examination of recent micro deliberative institutions.

Young, Iris M. (2000) *Inclusion and Democracy* (Oxford: Oxford University Press): presents an alternative, *communicative* version of deliberative democracy that puts great emphasis on equality and inclusion.

Edited Volumes

Macedo, Stephen (ed.) (1999) *Deliberative Politics: Essays on Democracy and Disagreement,* (Oxford: Oxford University Press): a collection of essays that respond to Gutmann and Thompson (1996).

Gastil, John and Peter Levine (2005) *The Deliberative Democracy Handbook: Strategies for Effective Civic Engagement in the Twenty-First Century* (San Francisco, CA: Jossey-Bass): a collection of papers that offers a good overview of deliberative methods used in practice.

Fung, Archon and Erik Olin Wright (eds) (2003) *Deepening Democracy: Institutional Innovations in Empowered Participatory Governance* (London: Verso): a collection of papers describing micro deliberation aimed at empowering citizens.

The following edited volumes cover a range of theoretical perspectives:

Benhabib, Seyla (ed.) (1996) *Democracy and Difference: Contesting the Boundaries of the Political* (Princeton, NJ: Princeton University Press).

Bohman, James and William Rehg (eds) (1997) *Deliberative Democracy: Essays on Reason and Politics* (Cambridge, MA: MIT Press).

Bibliography

Ackerman, Bruce A. (1991) *We the People* (Cambridge, MA: Harvard University Press).

Ackerman, Bruce A. and James Fishkin (2004) *Deliberation Day* (New Haven, CT: Yale University Press).

—— (2008) 'A Better Way with Referendums', *Financial Times,* 17 June 2008.

Aldrich, John H. (1993) 'Rational Choice and Turnout', *American Journal of Political Science,* 37 (1), 246–78.

Almond, Gabriel A. and Sidney Verba (1963) *The Civic Culture: Political Attitudes and Democracy in Five Nations* (Princeton, NJ: Princeton University Press).

—— (1989) *The Civic Culture: Political Attitudes and Democracy in Five Nations* (Newbury Park, CA: Sage).

Arrow, Kenneth J. (1951) *Social Choice and Individual Values* (London: Chapman & Hall).

—— (1963) *Social Choice and Individual Values* (New York, NY: Wiley).

Baiocchi, Gianpaolo (2003) 'Participation, Activism and Politics: The Porto Alegre Experiment', in Archon Fung and Erik Olin Wright (eds), *Deepening Democracy: Institutional Innovations in Empowered Participatory Governance* (London: Verso) pp. 45–76.

Barber, Benjamin R. (1984) *Strong Democracy: Participatory Politics for a New Age* (Berkeley, CA: University of California Press).

Barry, Brian (2002) 'Social Exclusion Social Isolation and the Distribution of Income', in Phil Agulnik, John Hills, Julian Le Grand and David Piachaud (eds), *Understanding Social Exclusion* (Oxford: Oxford University Press), pp. 13–29.

Bartels, Larry M. (1993) 'Messages Received', *American Political Science Review,* 87(2), 267–85.

Beitz, Charles (1989) *Political Equality: An Essay in Democratic Theory* (Princeton, NJ: Princeton University Press).

Benhabib, Seyla (1996) 'Toward a Deliberative Model of Democratic Legitimacy', in Seyla Benhabib (ed.), *Democracy and Difference: Contesting the Boundaries of the Political* (Princeton, NJ: Princeton University Press), pp. 67–94.

Besley, Timothy and Stephen Coate (1991) 'An Economic Model of Representative Democracy', *Quarterly Journal of Economics,* 112, 85–114.

173

Black, Duncan (1948) 'On The Rationale Of Group Decision-Making', *Journal of Political Economy,* 56, 23–34.

Bohman, James (1988) 'Emancipation and Rhetoric: The Perlocutions and Illocutions of the Social Critic', *Philosophy and Rhetoric,* 21(3), 185–203.

——— (1996) *Public Deliberation: Pluralism, Complexity, and Democracy* (Cambridge, MA: MIT Press).

——— (1997) 'Deliberative Democracy and Effective Social Freedom: Capabilities, Resources and Opportunities', in James Bohman and William Rehg (eds), *Deliberative Democracy: Essays on Reason and Politics* (Cambridge, MA: MIT Press), pp. 321–48.

——— (2003) 'Deliberative Toleration', *Political Theory,* 31(6), 757–79.

Bohman, James and William Rehg (eds) (1997) *Deliberative Democracy: Essays on Reason and Politics* (Cambridge, MA: MIT Press).

Bohman, James and Henry Richardson (2009) 'Liberalism, Deliberative Democracy, and "Reasons that All Can Accept"', *Journal of Political Philosophy,* 17(3), 253–74.

Bowler, Shaun, Todd Donovan and Jeffrey A. Karp (2006) 'Why Politicians Like Electoral Institutions: Self-interest, Values or Ideology?', *Journal of Politics,* 58(2), 434–46.

Brennan, Geoffrey and Robert E. Goodin (2001) 'Bargaining Over Beliefs', *Ethics,* 111(2), 256–77.

Brennan, Jason (2011) *The Ethics of Voting* (Princeton, NJ: Princeton University Press).

Bryan, Frank M. (2004) *Real democracy: the New England town meeting and how it works* (Chicago, IL: University of Chicago Press).

Burchardt, Tania, Julian le Grand and David Piachaud (2002) 'Degrees of Exclusion: Developing a Dynamic, Multidimensional Measure', in John Hills *et al.* (eds), *Understanding Social Exclusion* (Oxford: Oxford University Press), pp. 30–43.

Burke, Edmund ([1774] 1999) 'Speech to the Electors of Bristol', in E. J. Payne (ed.), *Select Works of Edmund Burke* (Liberty Fund).

Campbell, Angus, Philip E. Converse, Warren E. Miller and Donald E. Stokes (1960) *The American Voter* (New York, NY: Wiley).

Center for Deliberative Democracy (2012a) 'Deliberative Polling', http://cdd.stanford.edu/polls/index.html, accessed 19 January 2012.

Center for Deliberative Democracy (2012b) 'Deliberative Polling: European Union', http://cdd.stanford.edu/polls/eu/, accessed 19 January 2012.

Chambers, Simone (2004) 'Behind Closed Doors: Publicity, Secrecy, and the Quality of Deliberation', *Journal of Political Philosophy,* 12(4), 389–410.

Chappell, Zsuzsanna (2010) 'Formal and Informal Models of Deliberative Democracy: A Tension in the Theory of Political Deliberation', *Representation.* 46(3), 295–308.

—— (2011) 'Justifying Deliberative Democracy: Are Two Heads Always Wiser Than One?' *Contemporary Political Theory* 10(1), 78–101.

Christiano, Thomas (1996) *The Rule of the Many: Fundamental Issues in Democratic Theory* (Boulder, CO: Westview Press).

—— (2004) 'The Authority of Democracy', *Journal of Political Philosophy* 12(3), 266–290.

—— (2008) *The Constitution of Equality: Democratic Authority and Its Limits* (Oxford: Oxford University Press).

Cohen, Joshua (1986) 'An Epistemic Conception of Democracy', *Ethics* 97(1), 26–38.

—— (1989) 'Deliberation and Democratic Legitimacy', in Alan Hamlin and Philip Pettit (eds), *The Good Polity* (London: Blackwell) pp. 17–34.

—— (1995) 'Review of "Inequality Reexamined" by Amartya Sen', *Journal of Philosophy*, 92, 275–88.

—— (1996) 'Procedure and Substance in Deliberative Democracy', in Seyla Benhabib (ed.), *Democracy and Difference: Contesting the Boundaries of the Political* (Princeton, NJ: Princeton University Press), pp. 95–119.

—— (1997) 'Deliberation and Democratic Legitimacy', reprinted in James Bohman and William Rehg (eds), *Deliberative Democracy: Essays on Reason and Politics* (Cambridge, MA: MIT Press), pp. 67–92.

Cohen, Joshua and Joel Rogers (2003) 'Power and Reason', in Archon Fung and Erik Olin Wright (eds), *Deepening Democracy: Institutional Innovations in Empowered Participatory Governance*, (London: Verso), pp. 237–55.

Cohen, Robin (1987) *The New Helots: Migrants in the International Division of Labour* (Aldershot: Gower).

Condorcet, Jean-Antoine-Nicolas de Caritat ([1785] 1994) 'Essay on the Application of Analysis to the Probability of Majority Decisions', in Condorcet, Jean-Antoine-Nicolas de Caritat, Iain McLean and Fiona Hewitt, *Condorcet: Foundations of Social Choice and Political Theory* (Aldershot: Elgar).

Cox, Gary W. and Matthew D. McCubbins (1993) *Legislative Leviathan: Party Government in the House* (Berkeley, CA: University of California Press).

Cramer Walsh, Katherine (2004) *Talking About Politics* (Chicago, IL: University of Chicago Press).

Crosby, Ned and Doug Nethercut (2005) 'Citizens Juries: Creating a Trustworthy Voice of the People', in John Gastil and Peter Levine (eds), *The Deliberative Democracy Handbook: Strategies for Effective Civic Engagement in the Twenty-First Century* (San Francisco, CA: Jossey-Bass).

Cutler, Fred *et al.* (2008) 'Deliberation, Information, and Trust: The British Columbia Citizens' Assembly as Agenda Setter', in Mark E. Warren and Hilary Pearse (eds), *Designing Deliberative Democracy: The British Columbia Citizens' Assembly* (Cambridge: Cambridge University Press), pp. 166–91.

Dahl, Robert A. (1989) *Democracy and Its Critics* (New Haven, CT: Yale University Press).

—— (2006) *On Political Equality* (New Haven, CT: Yale University Press).

Delli Carpini, Michael X. and Scott Keeter (1996) *What Americans Know About Politics and Why It Matters* (New Haven, CT: Yale University Press).

De Tocqueville, Alexis (1835/1945) *Democracy in America* (New York, NY: Knopf).

Dietrich, Franz and Spiekermann, Kai (2010) 'Epistemic Democracy with Defensible Premises', London School of Economics Choice Group Working Papers, Volume 6.

Dowding, Keith (2005) 'Is it Rational to Vote? Five Types of Answer and a Suggestion', *British Journal of Politics and International Relations*, 7(3), 442–59.

Downs, Anthony (1957) *An Economic Theory of Democracy* (New York, NY: Harper and Row).

Dryzek, John S. (1990) *Discursive Democracy: Politics, Policy, and Science* (Cambridge: Cambridge University Press).

—— (1996) *Democracy in Capitalist Times: Ideals, Limits, and Struggles* (Oxford: Oxford University Press).

—— (2000) *Deliberative Democracy and Beyond: Liberals, Critics, Contestations* (Oxford: Oxford University Press).

—— (2006) *Deliberative Global Politics* (Oxford: Polity).

Dryzek, John. S. and Valerie Braithwaite (2000) 'On the Prospects for Democratic Deliberation: Values Analysis Applied to Australian Politics', *Political Psychology*, 21(2), 241–66.

Dryzek, John S. and Christian List (2003) 'Social Choice Theory and Deliberative Democracy: A Reconciliation', *British Journal of Political Science*, 33(1), 1–28.

Dryzek, John S. and Simon Niemeyer (2008) 'Discursive Representation', *American Political Science Review*, 102(4), 481–93.

Dunleavy, Patrick (1991) *Democracy, Bureaucracy and Public Choice: Economic Explanations in Political Science* (London: Prentice-Hall).

Dworkin, Ronald (1987) 'What is Equality – Part 4: Political Equality', *University of San Francisco Law Review*, 22(1), 1–30.

Electoral Commission and Hansard Society (2006) *An Audit of Political Engagement 3* (Hansard Society).

—— (2007) *An Audit of Political Engagement 4* (Hansard Society).

—— (2011) *An Audit of Political Engagement 8* (Hansard Society).

Elster, Jon (1986) 'The Market and the Forum: Three Varieties Of Political Theory', in Jon Elster and Aanund Hylland (eds), *Foundations Of Social Choice Theory* (Cambridge: Cambridge University Press), pp. 103–32.

—— (1989) *The Cement of Society: A Study of Social Order* (Cambridge: Cambridge University Press).

—— (1998) 'Introduction', in Jon Elster (ed.), *Deliberative Democracy* (Cambridge: Cambridge University Press), pp. 1–18.

Elstub, Stephen (2008) *Towards a Deliberative Democracy* (New York, NY: Columbia University Press).

Estlund, David (1997) 'Beyond Fairness and Deliberation: The Epistemic Dimension of Democratic Authority', in James Bohman and William Rehg (eds), *Deliberative Democracy: Essays on Reason and Politics* (Cambridge, MA: MIT Press), pp. 173–204.

—— (2008) *Democratic Authority: A Philosophical Framework* (Princeton, NJ: Princeton University Press).

Fang, Songying (2008) 'The Informational Role of International Institutions and Domestic Politics', *American Journal of Political Science,* 52(2), 304–21.

Farrar, Cynthia, James Fishkin, Donald Green, Christian List, Robert Luskin and Elizabeth Levy Paluck (2010) 'Disaggregating Deliberation's Effects: An Experiment Within a Deliberative Poll', *British Journal of Political Science*, 40(2), 333–47.

Fearon, James D. (1999) 'Electoral Accountability and the Control of Politicians: Electing Good Types versus Sanctioning Poor Performance', in Adam Przeworski, Susan Carol Stokes and Bernard Manin (eds), *Democracy, Accountability, and Representation* (Cambridge: Cambridge University Press), pp. 55–97.

Fiorina, Morris P. (1978) 'Economic Retrospective Voting in American National Elections: A Micro-Analysis', *American Journal of Political Science,* 22(2), 426–43.

—— (1981) *Retrospective Voting in American National Elections*, (New Haven, CT: Yale University Press).

Fish, Stanley (1999) 'Mutual Respect as a Device of Exclusion', in Stephen Macedo (ed.), *Deliberative Politics: Essays on Democracy and Disagreement* (Oxford: Oxford University Press), pp. 88–102.

Fishkin, James S. (1991) *Democracy and Deliberation: New Directions for Democratic Reform* (New Haven, CT: Yale University Press).

—— (2009) *When the People Speak: Deliberative Democracy and Public Consultation* (Oxford: Oxford University Press).

Fishkin, James S., Christian List, Robert C. Luskin and Iain McLean (2007) 'Deliberation, Single-Peakedness and the Possibility of Meaningful Democracy: Evidence from Deliberative Polls', unpublished manuscript.

Fishkin, James S., Robert C. Luskin and Roger Jowell (2002) 'Considered Opinions: Deliberative Polling in Britain', *British Journal of Political Science,* 32, 455–87.

Fraser, Nancy (1992) 'Rethinking The Public Sphere: A Contribution To The Critique Of Actually Existing Democracy', in Craig Calhoun (ed.), *Habermas and The Public Sphere* (Cambridge, MA: MIT Press), pp. 107–42.

Freedom House (2011) *Freedom in the World*, http://www.freedomhouse.org/ reports, accessed 19 January 2012.

Frohlich, Norman, Joe Oppenheimer and Anja Kurki (2004) 'Modeling Other-Regarding Preferences and an Experimental Test', *Public Choice,* 119(1–2), 91–117.

Fung, Archon (2003) 'Survey Article: Recipes for Public Spheres: Eight Institutional Design Choices and Their Consequences', *Journal of Political Philosophy,* 11(3), 338–67.

—— (2004) *Empowered Participation: Reinventing Urban Democracy* (Princeton, NJ: Princeton University Press).

Fung, Archon and Erik Olin Wright (2003) 'Thinking About Empowered Participatory Governance', in Archon Fung and Erik Olin Wright (eds), *Deepening Democracy: Institutional Innovations in Empowered Participatory Governance* (London: Verso), pp. 3–42.

Gamson, William A. (1992) *Talking Politics* (Cambridge University Press).

Gastil, John (2000) *By Popular Demand: Revitalizing Representative Democracy Through Deliberative Elections* (Berkeley, CA: University of California Press).

Gastil, John and Peter Levine (2005) *The Deliberative Democracy Handbook: Strategies for Effective Civic Engagement in the Twenty-First Century* (San Francisco, CA: Jossey-Bass).

Gaus, Gerald F. (1999), 'Reason, Justification and Consensus: Why Democracy Can't Have It All', in James Bohman and William Rehg (eds), *Deliberative Democracy: Essays on Reason and Politics* (Cambridge, MA: MIT Press), pp. 205–42.

Gehrlein, William V. (2002) 'Condorcet's Paradox and the Likelihood of Its Occurrence: Different Perspectives on Balanced Preferences', *Theory and Decision,* 52(2), 171–99.

Gibbard, Allan (1973) 'Manipulation of Voting Schemes: A General Result', *Econometrica,* 41(4), 587–602.

Goodin, Robert (1986) 'Laundering Preferences', in Jon Elster and Aanund Hylland (eds), *Foundations Of Social Choice Theory* (Cambridge: Cambridge University Press).

—— (2003) *Reflective democracy* (Oxford: Oxford University Press).

—— (2008) *Innovating Democracy: Democratic Theory and Practice After the Deliberative Turn* (Oxford: Oxford University Press).

Goodin, Robert. E. and Simon J. Niemayer (2003) 'When Does Deliberation Begin? Internal Reflection versus Public Discussion in Deliberative Democracy', *Political Studies,* 51, 627–49.

Goodin, Robert. E. and K. W. S. Roberts (1975) 'The ethical voter', *American Political Science Review,* 69(3), 926–8.

Gret, Marion and Yves Sintomer (2005) *The Porto Alegre experiment: learning lessons for better democracy* (London: Zed Books).

Grofman, Bernard, Guillermo Owen and Scott L. Feld (1983) 'Thirteen Theorems in Search of the Truth', *Theory and Decision,* 15(3), 261–78.

Grofman, Bernard and Julie Withers (1993) 'Information-pooling Models of Electoral Politics', in Bernard Grofman (ed.), *Information, Participation, And Choice: An Economic Theory Of Democracy In Perspective* (Ann Arbor, MI: University of Michigan Press), pp. 55–64.

Gutmann, Amy and Dennis Thompson (1996) *Democracy and disagreement* (Cambridge, MA: Belknap Press).

—— (1999) 'Democratic Disagreement', in Stephen Macedo (ed.), *Deliberative Politics: Essays on Democracy and Disagreement* (Oxford: Oxford University Press), pp. 243–79.

—— (2004) *Why Deliberative Democracy?* (Princeton, NJ: Princeton University Press).

Habermas, Jürgen (1984) *The Theory of Communicative Action* (London: Heinemann Education).

—— (1985) 'Remarks on the Concept of Communicative Action', in Gottfried Seebass and Raimo Tuomela (eds), *Social Action, (*Dordrecht: D. Reidel), pp. 151–78.

—— (1996a) *Between Facts And Norms: Contributions to a Discourse Theory of Law and Democracy*, (Oxford: Polity).

—— (1996b) 'Three Normative Models of Democracy', in Seyla Benhabib (ed.), *Democracy and Difference: Contesting the Boundaries of the Political* (Princeton, NJ: Princeton University Press), pp. 21–30.

—— (2003) *Truth and Justification* (Cambridge, MA: MIT Press).

Hastie, Reid, Steven D. Penrod and Nancy Pennington (1983) *Inside the Jury* (Cambridge, MA: Harvard University Press).

He, Baogang and Leib, Ethan J. (2006) *The Search for Deliberative Democracy in China* (New York, NY: Palgrave Macmillan).

Heath, Joseph (2001) *Communicative Action and Rational Choice* (Cambridge, MA: MIT Press).

Hendriks, Carolyn M. (2005) 'Consensus Conferences and Planning Cells: Lay Citizen Deliberations', in John Gastil and Peter Levine (eds), *The Deliberative Democracy Handbook: Strategies for Effective Civic Engagement in the Twenty-First Century* (San Francisco, CA: Jossey-Bass).

—— (2006) 'Integrated Deliberation: Reconciling Civil Society's Dual Role in Deliberative Democracy', *Political Studies,* 54(3), 486–508.

Hibbing, John R. and Elizabeth Theiss-Morse (2002) *Stealth Democracy: Americans' Beliefs About How Government Should Work* (Cambridge: Cambridge University Press).

Hoffman, Elizabeth, Kevin McCabe and Vernon L. Smith (1996) 'Social Distance and Other-Regarding Behavior in Dictator Games', *The American Economic Review,* 86(3), 653–60.

Honig, Bonnie (1993) *Political Theory and the Displacement of Politics* (Ithaca, NY: Cornell University Press).

Huntington, Samuel P. (1996) *The Clash of Civilizations and the Remaking of World Order* (New York, NY: Simon and Schuster).

Husted, Thomas A. and Lawrence W. Kenny (1997) 'The Effect of the Expansion of the Voting Franchise on the Size of Government', *Journal of Political Economy,* 105, 54–82.

Isaac, Thomas and Patrick Heller (2003) 'Democracy and Development: Decentralised Planning in Kerala', in Archon Fung and Erik Olin Wright (eds), *Deepening Democracy: Institutional Innovations in Empowered Participatory Governance* (London: Verso), pp. 45–76.

Jackman, Robert. W. and Ross A. Miller (1998) 'Social Capital and Politics', *Annual Review of Political Science,* 1, 47–73.

Johnson, James (1998) 'Arguing for Deliberation: Some Skeptical Considerations', in Jon Elster (ed.), *Deliberative Democracy* (Cambridge: Cambridge University Press), pp. 161–84.

Kahnemann, Daniel and Amos Tversky (1979) 'Prospect Theory: An Analysis Of Decision Under Risk', *Econometrica,* 47(2), 263–91.

—— (1984) 'Choices, Values and Frames', *American Psychologist,* 39(4), 341–50.

Karpowitz, Christopher K. and Jane Mansbridge (2005) 'Disagreement and Consensus: The Importance of Dynamic Updating in Public Deliberation', in John Gastil and Peter Levine (eds), *The Deliberative Democracy Handbook: Strategies for Effective Civic Engagement in the Twenty-First Century* (San Francisco, CA: Jossey-Bass), pp. 237–53.

Knight, Jack and James Johnson (1994) 'Aggregation and Deliberation: On the Possibility of Democratic Legitimacy', *Political Theory,* 22(2), 277–96.

—— (1997) 'What Sort of Political Equality Does Deliberative Democracy Require?' in James Bohman and William Rehg (eds), *Deliberative Democracy: Essays on Reason and Politics* (Cambridge, MA: MIT Press), pp. 279–320.

Kymlicka, Will (1995) *Multicultural Citizenship: A Liberal Theory of Minority Rights* (Oxford: Oxford University Press).

Lang, Amy (2008) 'Agenda-setting in Deliberative Forums: Expert Influence and Citizen Autonomy in the British Columbia Citizens' Assembly', in Mark E. Warren and Hilary Pearse (eds), *Designing Deliberative Democracy: The British Columbia Citizens' Assembly* (Cambridge: Cambridge University Press), pp. 85–104.

Laver, Michael and Kenneth A. Shepsle (1995) *Making and Breaking Governments: Cabinets and Legislatures in Parliamentary Democracies* (Cambridge: Cambridge University Press).

Leach, William D. and Paul A. Sabatier (2005) 'To Trust an Adversary: Integrating Rational and Psychological Models of Collaborative Policymaking', *American Political Science Review,* 99(04), 491–503.

Leib, Ethan J. (2004) *Deliberative Democracy in America: A Proposal for a Popular Branch of Government* (University Park, PA: Pennsylvania State University Press).

Lever, Annabelle (2010) 'Compulsory Voting: A Critical Perspective', *British Journal of Political Science,* 40(4), 897–915.

Levine, John. M. and Richard L. Moreland (1990) 'Progress in Small Group Research', *Annual Review of Psychology,* 41, 585–634.

Lewin, Irwin. P. and Gary J. Gaeth (1988) 'How Consumers are Affected by the Framing of Attribute Information Before and After Consuming the Product', *Journal of Consumer Research,* 15(3), 374–8.

Lipset, Seymour M. (1959) 'Some Social Requisites of Democracy: Economic Development and Political Legitimacy', *American Political Science Review,* 53(1), 69–105.

List, Christian (2004) 'Substantive and Meta-Agreement', in Anne Van Aaken, Christian List and Christoph Luetge (eds), *Deliberation and Decision: Economics, Constitutional Theory and Deliberative Democracy* (Aldershot: Ashgate), pp. 119–34.

—— (2006) 'The Discursive Dilemma and Public Reason', *Ethics,* 116(2), 362–402.

List, Christian and Philip Pettit (2002) 'Aggregating Sets of Judgments: An Impossibility Result', *Economics and Philosophy,* 18, 89–110.

Locke, John (1988) *Two Treatises of Government* (Cambridge: Cambridge Univeristy Press).

Lupia, Arthur (2002) 'Deliberation Disconnected: What It Takes to Improve Civic Competence', *Law and Contemporary Problems,* 65(3), 133–50.

Macedo, Stephen (ed.) (1999) *Deliberative Politics: Essays on Democracy and Disagreement* (Oxford: Oxford University Press).

McCrae, Robert R. and Costa, Paul T. (2003) *Personality in Adulthood: A Five-Factor Theory Perspective* (New York, NY: Guilford Press).

Magyar Agora (2005) http://www.magyaragora.hu/, accessed 19 January 2012.

Manin, Bernard (1987) 'On Legitimacy and Political Deliberation', *Political Theory,* 15(3), 338–68.

—— (1997) *The Principles of Representative Government* (Cambridge: Cambridge University Press).

Mansbridge, Jane J. (1980) *Beyond Adversary Democracy* (New York, NY: Basic Books).

—— (1990) *Beyond Self-Interest* (Chicago, IL: University of Chicago Press).

—— (1999a) 'Should Blacks Represent Blacks and Women Represent Women? A Contingent "Yes"', *The Journal of Politics,* 61(3), 628–57.

—— (1999b) 'Everyday Talk in the Deliberative System', in Stephen Macedo (ed.), *Deliberative Politics: Essays on Democracy and Disagreement* (Oxford: Oxford University Press), pp. 211–39.

—— (2003) 'Rethinking Representation', *American Political Science Review*, 97(4), 515–28.

Mansbridge, Jane J. *et al.* (2010) 'The Place of Self-Interest and the Role of Power in Deliberative Democracy', *The Journal of Political Philosophy*, 18(1), 64–100.

May, Kenneth (1952) 'A set of independent necessary and sufficient conditions for simple majority decision', *Econometrica*, 20(4), 680–4.

Meltzer, Allan H. and Scott F. Richard (1981) 'A Rational Theory of the Size of Government', *The Journal of Political Economy*, 89(5), 914–27.

Meyerowitz, Beth E. and Shelly Chaiken, S. (1987) 'The Effect Of Message Framing On Breast Self-Examination Attitudes, Intentions, And Behaviour', *Journal of Personality and Social Psychology*, 52 (3), 500–10.

Miller, David (1992) 'Deliberative Democracy and Social Choice', *Political Studies*, 40, 54–67.

Misak, Cheryl J. (2000) *Truth, Politics, Morality: Pragmatism and Deliberation* (London: Routledge).

Mouffe, Chantal (1993) *The Return of the Political* (London: Verso).

—— (1996) 'Democracy, Power and the "Political"', in Seyla Benhabib (ed.), *Democracy and Difference: Contesting the Boundaries of the Political* (Princeton, NJ: Princeton University Press), pp. 245–56.

—— (2005) *On the Political: Thinking in Action* (Abingdon: Routledge).

Mueller, Dennis C. (2003) *Public Choice III* (Cambridge: Cambridge University Press).

Mutz, Diana C. (2006) *Hearing the Other Side: Deliberative Versus Participatory Democracy* (Cambridge: Cambridge University Press).

New Democracy (2009) *Citizens' Parliament: Final Report*, http://www.newdemocracy.com.au.

Niemi, Richard G. (1969) 'Majority Decision-Making with Partial Unidimensionality', *The American Political Science Review*, 63 (2), 488–97

Nino, Carlos S. (1996) *The Constitution Of Deliberative Democracy* (New Haven, CT: Yale University Press).

Niskanen, William A. (1971) *Bureaucracy And Representative Government* (Chicago, IL: Aldine).

Ober, Josiah (2008) *Democracy and Knowledge: Innovation and Learning in Classical Athens* (Princeton, NJ: Princeton University Press).

O'Donnell, Guillermo (1994) 'Delegative democracy', *Journal of Democracy*, 5, 55–69.

OECD (2007) *International Migration Outlook* (OECD).

O'Flynn, Ian (2006) *Deliberative Democracy and Divided Societies* (Edinburgh: Edinburgh University Press).

Olson, Mancur (1965) *The Logic of Collective Action: Public Goods and the Theory of Groups* (Cambridge, MA: Harvard University Press).

Ostrom, Elinor (1990) *Governing the Commons: The Evolution of Institutions for Collective Action* (Cambridge: Cambridge University Press).

Parkinson, John (2003) 'Legitimacy Problems in Deliberative Democracy', *Political Studies,* 51(1), 180–96.

—— (2006), *Deliberating in the real world: Problems of legitimacy in deliberative democracy* (Oxford: Oxford University Press).

PB Unit (2012) 'PB Unit Home Page', http://www.participatorybudgeting. org.uk/, accessed 19 January 2012.

Pellizzoni, Luigi (2001) 'The Myth of the Best Argument: Power, Deliberation and Reason', *British Journal of Sociology,* 52(1), 59–86.

Perrin, Andrew J. (2006) *Citizen Speak: The Democratic Imagination in American Life* (Chicago, IL: University of Chicago Press).

Peter, Fabienne (2007a) 'Democratic Legitimacy and Proceduralist Social Epistemology', *Politics, Philosophy and Economics*, 6(3), 329–53.

—— (2007b) 'The Political Egalitarian's Dilemma', *Ethical Theory and Moral Practice,* 10(4), 373–87.

Phillips, Anne (1995) *The Politics of Presence* (Oxford: Oxford University Press).

Pincione, Guido and Fernando R. Tesón (2006) *Rational Choice and Democratic Deliberation: A Theory of Discourse Failure* (Cambridge: Cambridge University Press).

Popkin, Samuel L. (1993) 'Information Shortcuts and the Reasoning Voter', in Bernard Grofman (ed.), *Information, Participation, and Choice: An Economic Theory of Democracy in Perspective* (Ann Arbor, MI: University of Michigan Press), pp. 17–36.

Putnam, Robert D. (2000) *Bowling Alone: The Collapse and Revival of American Community* (New York, NY: Simon & Schuster).

Rawls, John (1972) *A Theory of Justice* (Oxford: Clarendon Press).

—— (1987) 'The Idea of Overlapping Consensus', *Oxford Journal of Legal Studies,* 7(1), 1–25.

—— (1993) *Political Liberalism* (New York, NY: Columbia University Press).

—— (1997) 'The Idea of Public Reason Revisited', *The University of Chicago Law Review,* 64(3), 765–807.

Ray, James L. (1998) 'Does Democracy Cause Peace?' *Annual Review of Political Science,* 1, 27–46.

Reykowski, Janusz (2006) 'Deliberative Democracy and "Human Nature": An Empirical Approach', *Political Psychology,* 27(3), 323–46.

Riker, William H. (1982) *Liberalism Against Populism: A Confrontation Between the Theory of Democracy and the Theory of Social Choice* (Oxford: Freeman).

Rousseau, Jean-Jacques (1997) *The Social Contract and Other Later Political Writings* (Cambridge: Cambridge University Press).

Rueschemeyer, Dietrich, Evelyn Huber Stephens and John D. Stephens (1992) *Capitalist Development and Democracy* (Cambridge: Polity).

Rustow, Dankwart A. (1970) 'Transitions to Democracy: Toward a Dynamic Model', *Comparative Politics*, 2(3), 337–63.

Sanders, Lynn M. (1997) 'Against Deliberation', *Political Theory*, 25(3), 347–76.

Satterthwaite, Mark A. (1975) 'Strategy-Proofness and Arrow's Conditions', *Journal of Economic Theory*, 10, 187–217.

Saward, Michael (2003) 'Enacting Democracy', *Political Studies*, 51(1), 161–79.

Schattschneider, E. E. (1960) *The Semisovereign People: A Realist's View of Democracy in America*, (New York, NY: Holt, Rinehart & Winston).

Scheufele, Dietram A. and Dhavan V. Shah (2000) 'Personality Strength and Social Capital: The Role of Dispositional and Informational Variables in the Production of Civic Participation', *Communication Research*, 27(2), 107–31.

Schumpeter, Joseph A. (1976) *Capitalism, Socialism and Democracy* (London: Allen & Unwin).

Sen, Amartya K. (1970) *Collective Choice and Social Welfare* (San Francisco, CA: Holden-Day).

—— (1982) *Poverty and Famines: An Essay on Entitlements and Deprivation*, (Oxford: Clarendon Press).

—— (1992) *Inequality Reexamined* (Oxford: Oxford University Press).

—— (2000) *Social Exclusion: Concept, Application, and Scrutiny* (Asian Development Bank).

Sharot, Tali, Christoph W. Korn and Raymond J. Dolan (2011) 'How unrealistic optimism is maintained in the face of reality', *Nature Neuroscience*, 14, 1475–9.

Silk, Joan B., Sarah F. Brosnan, Jennifer Vonk, Joseph Henrich, Daniel J. Povinelli, Amanda S. Richardson, Susan P. Lambeth, Jenny Mascaro and Steven J. Schapiro (2005) 'Chimpanzees Are Indifferent to the Welfare of Unrelated Group Members', *Nature*, 437(27), 1357–9.

Skidmore, Paul and Kirsten Bound (2008) *The Everyday Democracy Index* (London: Demos).

Smith, Graham (2009) *Democratic Innovations: Designing Institutions for Citizen Participation* (Cambridge: Cambridge University Press).

Smith, Graham and Corinne Wales (2000) 'Citizens' Juries and Deliberative Democracy', *Political Studies*, 48, 51–65.

Souza, Celine (2001) 'Participatory Budgeting in Brazilian Cities: Limits and Possibilities in Building Democratic Institutions', *Environment and Urbanization*, 13(1), 159–84.

Squires, Judith (2002) 'Deliberation and Decision-Making: Discontinuities in the Two-Track Model', in Maurizio Passerin d'Entrèves (ed.),

Democracy as Public Deliberation: New Perspectives (Manchester: Manchester University Press), pp. 133–56.

Steiner, Jürg, André Bächtiger, Markus Spörndli and Marco R. Steenbergen (2003) 'Measuring Political Deliberation: A Discourse Quality Index', *Comparative European Politics* 1(1), 21–48.

—— (2004) *Deliberative Politics in Action: Analysing Parliamentary Discourse* (Cambridge: Cambridge University Press).

Sullivan, J. L. and J. E. Transue (1999) 'The Psychological Underpinnings of Democracy: A Selective Review of Research on Political Tolerance, Interpersonal Trust, and Social Capital', *Annual Review of Psychology,* 50, 625–50.

Sunstein, Cass R. (1994) 'Political Conflict and Legal Agreement', The Tanner Lectures on Human Values.

—— (2002) 'The Law Of Group Polarization', *Journal of Political Philosophy,* 10(2), 175–95.

—— (2003) *Why Societies Need Dissent* (Cambridge, MA: Harvard University Press).

—— (2007) *Republic.com 2.0* (Princeton, NJ: Princeton University Press).

Talisse, Robert. B. (2005) *Democracy After Liberalism: Pragmatism and Deliberative Politics* (London: Routledge).

Thompson, Dennis (2008) 'Deliberative Democratic Theory and Empirical Political Science', *Annual Review of Political Science,* 11, 497–520.

Tsebelis, George (2002) *Veto Players: How Political Institutions Work* (Princeton, NJ: Princeton University Press).

Tuck, Richard (2008) *Free Riding* (Cambridge, MA: Harvard University Press).

University of Groningen (2010) 'Sub-project 1: Deliberative polling and neighbourhood safety', http://www.philos.rug.nl/~olivier/SCCK/?body= sub1, accessed 19 January 2012.

Urbinati, Nadia (2006) *Representative Democracy: Principles and Genealogy* (Chicago, IL: University of Chicago Press).

Varian, Hal R. (1999) *Intermediate Microeconomics: A Modern Approach* (New York, NY: W.W. Norton & Co.).

Verba, Sidney, Kay Lehman Schlozman and Henry E. Brady (1995) *Voice and Equality: Civic Voluntarism in American Politics* (Cambridge, MA: Harvard University Press).

Von Neumann, John and Oskar Morgenstern (1947) *Theory of Games and Economic Behavior*, (Princeton, NJ: Princeton University Press).

Walker, Alison, Joanne Maher, Melissa Coulthard, Eileen Goddard and Margaret Thomas (2001) *Living in Britain: Results From the 2000/01 General Household Survey* (London: Stationery Office).

Warren, Mark E. and Hilary Pearse (2008) 'Introduction: Democratic Renewal and Deliberative Democracy', in Mark E. Warren and Hilary

Pearse (eds), *Designing Deliberative Democracy: The British Columbia Citizens' Assembly* (Cambridge: Cambridge University Press), pp. 1–19.

Williams, Melissa S. (1998) *Voice, Trust, and Memory: Marginalized Groups and the Failings of Liberal Representation* (Princeton, NJ: Princeton University Press).

Wright, Scott (2006) 'Government-Run Online Discussion Fora: Moderation, Censorship and the Shadow of Control', *The British Journal of Politics and International Relations,* 8(4), 550–68.

Young, Iris M. (1996) 'Communication and the Other: Beyond Deliberative Democracy', in Seyla Benhabib (ed.), *Democracy and Difference: Contesting the Boundaries of the Political* (Princeton, NJ: Princeton University Press), pp. 120–35.

—— (2000) *Inclusion and Democracy* (Oxford: Oxford University Press).

—— (2001) 'Activist Challenges to Deliberative Democracy', *Political Theory,* 29 (5), 670–90.

—— (2004) 'Modest Reflections on Hegemony and Global Democracy', *Theoria,* 51 (103), 1–14.

Zakaria, Fareed (1997) 'The Rise of Illiberal Democracy', *Foreign Affairs,* 76(6), 22–43.

Index

187